# BERRY LVERS COOK BOOK

Compiled by

Lee & Shayne K. Fischer

**GOLDEN WEST ☼ PUBLISHERS**

Front cover photo courtesy Oregon Raspberry and
    Blackberry Commission
Original berry art by Shayne K. Fischer

# Acknowledgments

The editors gratefully acknowledge the assistance and
cooperation of the following berry organizations and
growers: Gingerich Farms, Oregon Raspberry & Black-
berry Commission, Oregon Strawberry Commission, Berry
Works, Hurst's Berry Farm, Wisconsin Berry Growers
Association, Wild Blueberry Association of North America,
California Strawberry Commission, University of Illinois
at Urbana-Champaign, Florida Strawberry Festival,
Florida Strawberry Growers Association, North Carolina
Department of Agriculture, North Carolina Blueberry
Council, North American Blueberry Council, Michigan
Blueberry Growers Association. For addresses and
websites, see page 93.

Printed in the United States of America

Second Printing © 2000

ISBN #1-885590-81-4

**Golden West Publishers, Inc.**
4113 N. Longview Ave.
Phoenix, AZ 85014, USA

(602) 265-4392

Visit our website: http://www.goldenwestpublishers.com

# Berry Lovers Cook Book

## TABLE OF CONTENTS

### Blueberries

### Strawberries

## **Table of Contents** (Continued)

# **Raspberries**

# **Blackberries**

## Table of Contents (Continued)

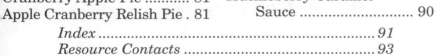

# Introduction

The next time you pop some fresh berries, bursting with flavor, into your mouth, you will not only be doing something good for your tastebuds, you will be doing something good for your health! Berries are known as neutraceuticals, meaning they are foods which serve specific benefits to human health.

Berries contain vitamins A and C, potassium, magnesium and iron. Berries have been shown to be major sources of antioxidant nutrients which help to prevent or delay degenerative diseases of aging, including cancer, cardiovascular disease and cataracts. Antioxidants help to fight off "free radicals" from smog, cigarette smoke and other pollutants. Ongoing research is showing that the types of berries featured in *Berry Lovers Cook Book* provide these benefits. In this day and age, when there is so much attention being focused on natural remedies, it is comforting to know that some of the tastiest foods available are also good for us!

This book is for the millions of people who enjoy eating and cooking berries. All across North America, families are creating and sharing traditional favorites and new special delights. Today's markets have some type of berries available year-round and pick-your-own farm markets have flourished, as we get back to nature.

*Berry Lovers Cook Book* will be a handy guide to baking your family favorites and will provide many tempting options on ways to utilize all those excess berries you enthusiastically lug home from the farm market!

The recipes in *Berry Lovers Cook Book* have been provided by berry councils, associations, growers and families across the country. While just the tip of the iceberg regarding the endless cooking and baking variations with berries, they are some of the best recipes for enjoying these natural wonders. We hope you have as much fun with these recipes as we have and that all your creations will be *berrylicious!*

# Blueberries

# Blueberries
# with
# Chicken Pasta Salad

**3 cups SPIRAL PASTA**
**1 cup PEA PODS, trimmed, cut in half**
**2 cups cubed, cooked CHICKEN**
**1 cup sliced CELERY**
**1 cup fresh BLUEBERRIES**
**1/2 cup finely chopped RED BELL PEPPER**
**1/4 cup chopped RED ONION**
**1/4 cup RED WINE VINEGAR**
**2-3 Tbsp. chopped fresh BASIL**
**SALT and PEPPER to taste**
**1 cup RED WINE VINEGAR DRESSING**
**1/2 cup freshly grated PARMESAN CHEESE**

Cook pasta according to directions on package. About 1 minute before it is cooked, add pea pods along with remaining ingredients except Parmesan cheese and dressing. Toss pasta mixture with 1/2 cup dressing. Cover and refrigerate several hours or overnight to blend flavors. Before serving, toss with remaining dressing and Parmesan cheese.

*When buying blueberries from the store, look for berries that are firm and plump. Berries should be free of stems and leaves. Moisture causes berries to mold so fruit should be dry. The berries should be a uniform blue color. Reddish berries are not ripe but are acceptable for use in baking. Berries stored for too long will begin to look shriveled or wrinkled from dehydration.*

# Red, White & Blueberry Cheese Spread

2 pkgs. (8 oz. ea.) CREAM CHEESE, softened
2 Tbsp. COINTREAU or TRIPLE SEC
1 Tbsp. LEMON JUICE
1/4 tsp. SEASONED SALT
1 Tbsp. HONEY
1 cup crushed PINEAPPLE, drained
1/3 cup BLUEBERRIES
1 cup chopped RED BELL PEPPER

Beat cream cheese in a mixing bowl. Add all ingredients except chopped red peppers, mix well. Place cheese mixture on center of a piece of plastic wrap. Bring corners up to meet and seal around cheese, molding mixture into a ball. Refrigerate overnight. Remove from refrigerator and form once again into a ball. Mixture will be stiff and easy to form. Roll cheese ball in finely chopped red peppers to cover. Garnish with fresh herbs and blueberries. Serve with crackers.

Makes 1 (16 oz.) ball.

# Blueberry & Tortellini Fruit Salad

1 pkg. (9 oz.) THREE CHEESE
    TORTELLINI PASTA
1 cup fresh BLUEBERRIES
1 cup sliced fresh
    STRAWBERRIES

3/4 cup GREEN GRAPES
1/4 sliced ALMONDS
1 can (11 oz.) MANDARIN
    ORANGE segments, drained
1/2 cup POPPY SEED DRESSING

Cook pasta according to directions on package; drain. In a large bowl, add pasta and salad ingredients. Pour dressing over salad and toss lightly; refrigerate until ready to serve.

Serves 6.

# Blueberry Raspberry Swirl Soup

**1 1/4 cups fresh BLUEBERRIES**
**1/2 cup BUTTERMILK**
**1/2 cup PLAIN NON FAT YOGURT**
**1 pkg. (10 oz.) unsweetened FROZEN RASPBERRIES, thawed**
**1/2 cup VANILLA FLAVORED NON FAT YOGURT**

Place 1 cup blueberries in blender and process until very smooth. Pour through a strainer to remove skins. To strained blueberries, add buttermilk and plain yogurt, stirring to mix well. Refrigerate until thoroughly chilled. Place raspberries in a strainer. With the back of a spoon, press berries to remove juice and pulp. Discard seeds. Stir 1/2 cup vanilla yogurt into raspberries. Refrigerate until thoroughly chilled. To serve the soup, divide the blueberry mixture among two bowls. Divide the raspberry mixture in half and carefully add to one side of the blueberry mixture in each bowl. With the tip of a knife, swirl the blueberry and raspberry together. Garnish the soup with the remaining 1/4 cup blueberries.

Serves 2.

### Freezing Blueberries

*Blueberries can be frozen right in the pint container they are normally packaged in. Wrap the entire container in plastic wrap being careful to cover all holes. Another easy way to freeze berries is to arrange them in a single layer on a cookie sheet and place in the freezer. When frozen, transfer the blueberries to a freezer container or freezer bag.*

# Glazed Blueberry Breakfast Rolls

**VEGETABLE COOKING SPRAY**
**3/4 cup finely chopped BLUEBERRIES**
**2 Tbsp. ORANGE JUICE**
**2 Tbsp. SUGAR**
**2 tsp. CORNSTARCH**
**1 1/2 tsp. grated ORANGE PEEL**
**1 can (10 oz.) refrigerated PIZZA CRUST DOUGH**
**FLOUR**
**1/2 cup POWDERED SUGAR**
**1 Tbsp. MILK**

Preheat oven to 375°. Coat 12 muffin cups with vegetable cooking spray. In a small saucepan, combine blueberries, orange juice, sugar, cornstarch and 1 tsp. grated orange peel, stirring to dissolve cornstarch. Cook over medium heat, stirring constantly until thick and bubbly (about 3 minutes). Set aside to cool for 10 minutes. Unroll pizza dough onto a lightly floured surface; pat into a 12 x 9 rectangle. Spread blueberry filling over dough, leaving a 1/2-inch border along the sides. Beginning with a long side, roll up jelly-roll fashion; pinch seam to seal (do not seal ends of roll). Cut roll into 12 (1-inch) slices. Place slices, cut side up, in coated muffin cups. Bake 12-15 minutes or until lightly browned. Remove rolls from pan; cool on a wire rack for at least 15 minutes before adding glaze. To make glaze: Combine powdered sugar, milk and 1/2 teaspoon grated orange peel; stir until smooth. Drizzle glaze over rolls.

Yields 12 rolls.

---

*Blueberries should be stored covered in the refrigerator.*
*Do not wash blueberries until just prior to use.*

# Blueberry Lemon Cheesecake Bars

1 cup BLUEBERRIES, chopped
1/4 cup ORANGE JUICE
2 Tbsp. SUGAR
2 tsp. CORNSTARCH

**Crumb Mixture:**
    1 1/4 cups FLOUR
    3/4 cup ROLLED OATS
    3/4 cup packed BROWN SUGAR
    1/2 cup chopped NUTS
    1/2 cup MARGARINE, chilled

1 pkg. (8 oz.) CREAM CHEESE, softened
2 EGGS
1/2 cup SUGAR
2 Tbsp. fresh LEMON JUICE
1 tsp. grated LEMON PEEL

Preheat oven to 350°. Lightly grease the bottom of a 13 x 9 pan. In a small saucepan, combine blueberries, orange juice, 2 tablespoons sugar and cornstarch; stir until cornstarch is dissolved. Cook over medium heat, stirring constantly until thick and bubbly (about 5 minutes). Set aside to cool slightly. In a large bowl, combine flour, oats, brown sugar and nuts. Mix well. Using a pastry blender or fork, cut in margarine until mixture resembles coarse crumbs. Reserve 1 cup crumb mixture for topping. Press remaining crumb mixture firmly in bottom of greased pan. Bake for 10 minutes. In a medium bowl, blend together cream cheese, eggs, 1/2 cup sugar, lemon juice and lemon peel with electric mixer on medium speed until well-blended; pour into baked crust. Spoon blueberry filling over cream cheese filling, swirl with a knife to blend. Sprinkle reserved crumb mixture over filling. Bake 20 to 25 minutes or until lightly browned.

Yields 36 bars.

# Blueberry Nut Loaves

2 cups FLOUR
2 tsp. BAKING POWDER
1/2 tsp. SALT
1 tsp. CINNAMON
1/2 cup BUTTER, room temperature
3/4 cup SUGAR
2 EGGS
1/2 cup MILK
2 Tbsp. LEMON JUICE
2 cups BLUEBERRIES
1/2 cup chopped WALNUTS or PECANS

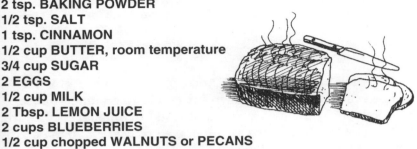

In a large bowl, mix flour, baking powder, salt and cinnamon. In a smaller bowl, cream butter and sugar. Beat in eggs and milk. Combine both mixtures until just moist. Pour lemon juice over blueberries and add berries and nuts to flour mixture. Pour into a greased 9 x 5 loaf pan. Bake at 350° for 1 hour.

# Blueberry Orange Loaves

1/2 cup BUTTER
3/4 cup SUGAR
2 EGGS
2 cups FLOUR
2 tsp. BAKING POWDER
1 tsp. CINNAMON
1 tsp. grated ORANGE PEEL
1/2 tsp. BAKING SODA
1/2 tsp. SALT
1/2 tsp. GROUND CLOVES
2/3 cup ORANGE JUICE
2 cups BLUEBERRIES
3/4 cup chopped PECANS

In a large bowl, beat butter and sugar until creamy. Add eggs one at a time. In a separate bowl, combine flour, baking powder, cinnamon, orange peel, baking soda, salt and cloves. Add this mixture to creamed mixture alternately with orange juice. Stir in blueberries and pecans. Pour mixture into 2 greased 8 x 4 loaf pans. Bake at 350° for 50 minutes.

# Smashing Blueberry Loaf

1/2 cup BUTTER
1 cup SUGAR
2 EGGS
2 cups fresh BLUEBERRIES
1 Tbsp. LEMON JUICE

2 cups FLOUR
3 Tbsp. BAKING POWDER
1/4 tsp. SALT
3/4 cup fresh BLUEBERRIES

Cream butter and sugar. Add eggs, beat until light. Purée 2 cups blueberries with lemon juice; add to creamed mixture. Sift flour, baking powder and salt. Add to blueberry mixture. Fold in 3/4 cup blueberries. Bake in a greased loaf pan at 375° for approximately 1 1/4 hours.

*When adding blueberries to batters avoid over-mixing as it may cause breakage and color bleeding.*

*To ripen blueberries faster, place them in a bag and add an apple.*

*One quart of blueberries weighs 1 1/2 pounds.*

# Blueberry Breakfast

12 slices FRENCH BREAD, cut into 1-inch cubes
16 oz. CREAM CHEESE, cubed
2 cups fresh or frozen BLUEBERRIES
12 lg. EGGS
1/3 cup MAPLE SYRUP
2 cups MILK

Place half of the bread cubes in a greased baking dish and scatter cream cheese over the top. Sprinkle cheese with blueberries and cover with remaining bread cubes. Blend eggs, syrup and milk and pour evenly over all. Cover tightly with foil; chill overnight. Cover and bake at 350° for 30 minutes; uncover and bake 30 minutes more. Serve with blueberry syrup.

Serves 6-8.

# Lemon Blueberry Biscuits

2 cups FLOUR
1/3 cup SUGAR
2 tsp. BAKING POWDER
1/2 tsp. BAKING SODA
1/4 tsp. SALT
8 oz. LEMON YOGURT
1 EGG, slightly beaten

1/4 cup BUTTER, melted
1 tsp. grated LEMON PEEL
2 cups fresh BLUEBERRIES
1/2 cup POWDERED SUGAR
1/2 tsp. grated LEMON PEEL
1 Tbsp. LEMON JUICE

In a large bowl, combine flour, sugar, baking powder, baking soda and salt. In another bowl, combine yogurt, egg, butter and 1 teaspoon lemon peel. Stir into dry ingredients just until moistened. Fold in blueberries. Drop by tablespoonful onto a greased baking sheet. Bake at 400° for 15-18 minutes or until lightly browned. For glaze, combine powdered sugar, grated lemon peel and lemon juice and drizzle over warm biscuits.

# Blueberry Buttermilk Muffins

2 1/2 cups FLOUR
2 1/2 tsp. BAKING POWDER
1/4 tsp. SALT
1 cup SUGAR
1 cup BUTTERMILK
2 EGGS, beaten
1/4 lb. BUTTER, melted and slightly browned
1 1/2 cups fresh or frozen BLUEBERRIES

Sift flour, baking powder, salt and sugar into a large bowl. Make a well, add buttermilk, eggs and melted butter. Mix well. Fold in blueberries. Fill well-greased muffin tins half full and bake at 400° for 20 minutes. Serve warm.

Yields 24 small muffins.

# Blueberry Corn Muffins

1 cup FLOUR
3/4 cup YELLOW CORNMEAL
1/4 cup SUGAR
1 1/2 tsp. BAKING POWDER
1/2 tsp. BAKING SODA
1/2 tsp. SALT

1 EGG
1/2 cup BUTTERMILK
1/2 cup BUTTER, melted
1 1/2 cups fresh or frozen
    BLUEBERRIES

Mix dry ingredients in a large bowl. Beat egg, buttermilk and melted butter in smaller bowl. Add to flour mixture and stir just until flour is moistened. Fold in blueberries. Spoon batter into greased muffin tins and bake at 425° 20-25 minutes until lightly browned. Serve warm.

Makes 12 muffins.

# Apple Blueberry Pie

3 cups peeled, sliced APPLES
1 cup fresh or frozen
    BLUEBERRIES
1 cup SUGAR

1 1/2 Tbsp. CORNSTARCH
1/2 tsp. CINNAMON
1 (8-inch) unbaked PIE CRUST

Combine apples, blueberries, sugar, cornstarch and cinnamon; mix well. Turn into pie crust and sprinkle with *Cheese Crumb Topping.* Bake in 425° oven 40-50 minutes or until apples are tender.

Makes 6 servings.

## Cheese Crumb Topping

1/2 cup shredded CHEDDAR
    CHEESE
1 cup FLOUR

2 Tbsp. SUGAR
3 Tbsp. BUTTER

Combine all ingredients; mix until crumbly.

# Blueberry Tart

**Crust:**
    1 3/4 cups FLOUR
    1/4 tsp. SALT
    1/2 cup HAZELNUTS, toasted and husked
    2 Tbsp. SUGAR
    1 tsp. CINNAMON
    1/2 cup plus 3 Tbsp. SWEET BUTTER
    1/4 cup ICE WATER

**Filling:**

| | |
|---|---|
| 2 pints fresh BLUEBERRIES | 2/3 cup SUGAR |
| 2 Tbsp. CORNSTARCH | 1/4 tsp. SALT |
| 1 Tbsp. TRIPLE SEC or | 1/4 tsp. CINNAMON |
| GRAND MARNIER | 1/4 tsp. MACE |
| 2 Tbsp. ORANGE JUICE | 1/2 Tbsp. SWEET BUTTER |

For crust, blend first 5 ingredients in food processor until nuts are finely ground. Add butter, cutting in by using on/off turns until mixture resembles a coarse meal. Mix in enough water to form moist clumps. Gather dough into a ball and flatten into a disk. Wrap in plastic. Chill for 1 hour. Rinse berries. Dry well and set aside. In a saucepan, dissolve cornstarch in liqueur and orange juice. Add berries, sugar, salt, cinnamon, mace and butter. Cook over medium heat until mixture starts to thicken, 4-5 minutes. Cool completely. Roll out dough between sheets of waxed paper to a 13-inch round. Transfer crust to a 9-inch tart pan. Pour cooled filling into crust. Scallop crust edge over berries. Brush crust with egg glaze (beat **1 EGG** with **1 teaspoon WATER**) and sprinkle entire tart with **2-3 tablespoons** of **SUGAR**. Bake in a preheated 400° oven for 30-35 minutes or until golden brown. Cool on wire rack.

### Dried Blueberries

*Blueberries retain their antioxidant benefits after dehydration. In fact, most dried blueberries have very high antioxidant levels.*

# Blueberry Buckle

1/2 cup SHORTENING
3/4 cup SUGAR
1 EGG
2 cups FLOUR
2 1/2 tsp. BAKING POWDER
1/4 tsp. SALT

1/2 cup MILK
2 cups fresh BLUEBERRIES
1/2 cup SUGAR
1/2 cup FLOUR
1/2 tsp. CINNAMON
1/4 cup MARGARINE

Thoroughly cream shortening and sugar; add egg and beat until light and fluffy. Sift together 2 cups flour, baking powder and salt. Add to creamed mixture alternately with milk. Spread in greased 11 x 7 x 2 pan; top with blueberries. Mix remaining sugar, flour and cinnamon. Cut in margarine until crumbly and sprinkle over berries. Bake at 350° for 45 minutes. Cut in squares and serve warm with ice cream or sweetened whipped cream.

# White Chocolate
# Berry Cluster

1 lb. WHITE CHOCOLATE, melting-type
1 cup DRIED BLUEBERRIES
3/4 cup UNSWEETENED SHREDDED COCONUT
1/2 cup chopped NUTS

Melt chocolate in pan over hot water (double boiler method). Do not let water come to a boil. When chocolate is completely melted, remove from heat. Stir in remaining ingredients immediately. Place by teaspoonful onto waxed paper. Let cool completely before removing.

Makes 24 (2-inch) clusters.

# Fruit Leather

**4 cups fresh BLUEBERRIES**
**1 cup fresh STRAWBERRIES, hulled**
**1/4 cup HONEY**
**1 Tbsp. ALMOND EXTRACT**

Place blueberries and strawberries in blender and blend until smooth. Pour mixture through a strainer to remove skin and seeds. Stir in honey and almond extract. Place mixture in a large skillet. While stirring frequently, cook over very low heat for 1 hour until thickened. Line a cookie sheet with parchment paper or aluminum foil. Preheat oven to 150°. Pour thickened mixture onto parchment paper and spread to form an 8 x 12 rectangle. Bake for 5 1/2 to 6 hours until the fruit sheet is dry enough not to stick to your fingers but moist enough to roll. Remove from oven and cool. Once cool, leather should be stored in an airtight container or rolled in plastic wrap to keep.

Note: (Placing a potholder in the oven door to keep it ajar will help dry the leather by allowing moisture to escape.)

Makes 6 (3 x 4-inch) squares.

# Blueberry Jam

**2 1/2 cups fresh BLUEBERRIES**
**3 cups SUGAR**
**1/2 bottle (3 oz.) FRUIT PECTIN**
**1/3 cup fresh ORANGE JUICE**
**1 Tbsp. fresh LEMON JUICE**

Wash and drain blueberries. Crush blueberries in an enamel or stainless steel pan. Add sugar, pectin and fruit juices. Mix well. Bring to a full rolling boil. Boil hard for 1 minute, stirring constantly. Remove from heat. Pour into hot, sterilized jars according to manufacturer's directions.

Makes 3 cups or 4 (6-ounce) jars.

# Blueberry Fruit Smoothie

1 cup LOW FAT VANILLA ICE CREAM
1 cup fresh or frozen BLUEBERRIES (do not thaw)
1/2 cup PEACHES, packed in water or natural juices, chopped
1/2 cup unsweetened PINEAPPLE JUICE
1/4 cup LOW FAT VANILLA YOGURT

Place all ingredients in a blender. Cover and mix until smooth, about 30 to 45 seconds.

Yields 2 servings.

 *Blueberries contain vitamins A and C, iron, potassium and magnesium. They are also a good source of carbohydrates and fiber, yet they are low in sodium and cholesterol-free.*

# Blueberry Graham Pudding

4 cups fresh BLUEBERRIES, rinsed and drained
1/2 cup SUGAR
3 Tbsp. FLOUR
2 tsp. grated ORANGE PEEL
1 EGG
1/4 cup SUGAR
1 tsp. grated ORANGE PEEL
1 cup GRAHAM CRACKER CRUMBS
1/4 cup finely chopped ALMONDS

Preheat oven to 350°. Combine berries, sugar, flour and 2 teaspoons orange peel. Pour mixture into a 1-quart baking dish. Combine remaining ingredients and blend well. Spoon mixture evenly over berries. Bake for 25 minutes or until crusty on top. Spoon into bowls and serve warm with ice cream.

# Blueberry Ice Cream

**1 env. UNFLAVORED GELATIN**
**1/2 cup COLD MILK**
**1/2 cup MILK, heated to boiling**
**2 cups fresh BLUEBERRIES**
**3/4 cup SUGAR**
**2 cups HEAVY CREAM, whipped**

In a 5-cup blender, sprinkle unflavored gelatin over cold milk. Let stand 3-4 minutes. Add hot milk and process at low speed until gelatin is completely dissolved, about 2 minutes. Let cool completely. Add blueberries and sugar, processing at a high speed until blended. Pour into a large bowl and chill, stirring occasionally, until mixture mounds slightly when dropped from a spoon. Fold whipped cream into gelatin mixture. Pour into two 4 x 10 freezer trays or an 8-inch baking pan. Freeze until firm.

Makes 1 1/2 quarts.

 *Blueberries contain only 42 calories per half-cup serving.*

# Blueberry Cheesecake

**1 1/2 cups SUGAR**
**3 pkgs. (8 oz. ea.) CREAM CHEESE, softened**
**4 EGGS**
**1 (10-inch) GRAHAM CRACKER CRUST**
**1 pint SOUR CREAM**
**1 tsp. VANILLA**
**1/2 cup SUGAR**
**2 cups fresh BLUEBERRIES, washed and drained**

Cream sugar and cream cheese. Add eggs, one at a time and beat well after each addition. Pour into graham cracker crust. Bake at 350° for 45 minutes. Let cool 15 minutes. While cheesecake is cooling, mix sour cream, vanilla and sugar in a large bowl. Fold in blueberries. Pour onto cake and bake at 450° for 10 minutes. Cool before serving.

# Blueberry Strawberry Mousse Pie

1 env. UNFLAVORED GELATIN
1/4 cup COLD WATER
2 Tbsp. LEMON JUICE
1 cup finely chopped fresh BLUEBERRIES
1 cup finely chopped fresh STRAWBERRIES
3/4 cup POWDERED SUGAR
1 ctn. (8 oz.) WHIPPED TOPPING
1 (9-inch) prepared GRAHAM CRACKER CRUMB CRUST

In a small saucepan, sprinkle gelatin over cold water; let stand 1 minute. Stir over low heat until gelatin is completely dissolved (about 1 minute). Stir in lemon juice; set aside to cool. In a large bowl, add blueberries, strawberries and powdered sugar; toss to coat. Stir in dissolved gelatin. Fold in whipped topping; spoon mixture into crust. Refrigerate 3-4 hours or until firm.

*The blueberry is a true blue food. It derives its coloring from the high content of anthocyanin, which is a water-soluble pigment that imparts colors ranging from blue to shades of red.*

# Blueberry Pie

1 qt. fresh BLUEBERRIES
4 Tbsp. WHOLE-WHEAT FLOUR
3/4 cup DATE SUGAR
1 Tbsp. SORGHUM
1/2 tsp. CINNAMON
1 (9-inch) unbaked PIE SHELL
3 Tbsp. flaked COCONUT

In large bowl, mix blueberries, flour, sugar, sorghum and cinnamon. Pour into unbaked pie shell and bake at 350° for 40-45 minutes. Garnish with coconut.

# Blueberry Banana Split Pie

3 cups GRAHAM CRACKER CRUMBS
3 sticks BUTTER
3 EGGS
1 box (1 lb.) POWDERED SUGAR
1 lg. can (20 oz.) crushed PINEAPPLE, drained and
    juice reserved
3-4 lg. BANANAS, sliced
1 pint fresh STRAWBERRIES
1 pint fresh BLUEBERRIES
1 ctn. (8 oz.) WHIPPED TOPPING
chopped PECANS
CHERRIES

Mix crumbs and 1 stick of melted butter. Press into a 9-inch pie pan. Beat eggs; add 2 sticks of softened butter and powdered sugar. Mix well and spread over crust. Top egg mixture with layers of pineapple, bananas, strawberries and blueberries. Top with whipped topping. Sprinkle with pecans and garnish with cherries. Chill and serve.

Note: To prevent bananas from darkening, slice them into the pineapple juice before adding to the mixture.

# Sweet Blueberry Pie

3 cups fresh BLUEBERRIES
1 cup SWEETENED CONDENSED
    MILK
1 cup SUGAR
1 1/2 Tbsp. LEMON JUICE
1 (8-inch) unbaked PIE
    SHELL
2 Tbsp. BUTTER

Mix blueberries, sweetened condensed milk, sugar and lemon juice. Pour into pie shell and dot with butter. Bake at 350° for 60 minutes or until done.

# Old-Fashioned Blueberry Pie

**Crust:**
- 1/4 cup ICE WATER
- 1 EGG YOLK
- 1 Tbsp. CIDER VINEGAR
- 2 cups FLOUR
- 1 stick BUTTER, softened

**2 pints fresh BLUEBERRIES**

**Filling:**
- 1 cup SUGAR
- 6 Tbsp. FLOUR
- 1/4 tsp. SALT
- 1/4 cup CINNAMON
- 1/4 tsp. MACE
- 1 1/2 tsp. finely grated LEMON PEEL
- 2 Tbsp. BUTTER, cut into small pieces

Mix water, egg yolk and vinegar together until well blended; set aside. Put 2 cups flour into a medium bowl, cut in one stick of butter with pastry blender until mixture resembles coarse crumbs. Stir in water mixture until mixture comes together to form a dough ball. Refrigerate 30 minutes before rolling. Rinse, pick over and dry the blueberries. Set aside. Sift together sugar, 6 tablespoons flour, salt, cinnamon and mace. Place the blueberries in a large bowl. Sprinkle lemon peel and 1/3 of the sugar mixture over the blueberries and toss. Roll out 1/2 of the pie crust dough into a circle. Line a 9-inch pie pan with dough. Fill pie pan with 1/2 blueberry mixture and 1/2 of remaining sugar mixture. Top with remaining blueberries and the rest of the sugar mixture. Dot with butter. Roll out remaining dough to make top crust. Cover berries with top crust. Seal and flute edges. Cut air vents into top with a sharp knife. Brush top with egg wash, if desired. Bake on lower rack of preheated 450° oven for 20 minutes. Lower oven temperature to 350° and continue baking 40 minutes.

# Blueberry Lattice-Top Pie

1 pkg. (11 oz.) PIE CRUST MIX
2 pints BLUEBERRIES
4 tsp. LEMON JUICE
1/2 cup FLOUR

1/2 tsp. CINNAMON
1 tsp. grated LEMON PEEL
3/4 cup SUGAR

Prepare pie crust according to package directions. Roll out 2/3 of the pie crust large enough to line the bottom and sides of an ungreased 9-inch pie pan. Reserve 1/4 cup of the blueberries for garnish. Sprinkle remaining berries with lemon juice. Mix remaining ingredients. Toss berries gently with dry mixture. Turn into pastry shell, heaping slightly in center. Roll out remaining pie crust and cut into 10 half-inch wide strips. Arrange strips in a lattice design over pie filling. Crimp or flute edges. Bake at 450° for 10 minutes. Reduce heat to 350° and bake 30 minutes or until crust is light golden brown. Cool. Garnish between lattices with reserved blueberries.

# Blueberry Pizza

1 1/4 cup POWDERED SUGAR
1 cup FLOUR
1/2 cup BUTTER, softened
1 pkg. (8 oz.) CREAM CHEESE, softened
1 tsp. VANILLA
1 ctn. (8 oz.) WHIPPED TOPPING
2 cups fresh BLUEBERRIES, washed and drained

In a medium bowl, mix together 1/4 cup powdered sugar, flour and butter to a soft dough. Spread the dough onto a 12-inch pizza pan and bake at 350° for 20 minutes or until golden. Let cool. In a large bowl, combine the cream cheese, remaining cup of powdered sugar and vanilla. Mix well, then fold in whipped topping. Spread mixture over the cooled crust; top with blueberries. Refrigerate for 2 hours before serving.

# Blueberry Turnovers

**Filling:**
- 1 cup WATER
- 1 cup SUGAR
- 1/8 tsp. SALT
- 2 1/2 cups fresh BLUEBERRIES
- 3 Tbsp. CORNSTARCH
- 4 Tbsp. WATER

**Dough:**
- 2 cups FLOUR
- 1/2 cup MILK
- 1 tsp. SALT

**Oil for frying**

Place first three filling ingredients in a saucepan and bring to a boil, stirring to dissolve the sugar. Add blueberries and bring to a boil. Dissolve cornstarch in water; stir into blueberry mixture. Cook until thickened and bubbly, stirring constantly. Remove from heat. Chill. Place flour, milk and 1 teaspoon salt in food processor; pulse several times to form a ball of dough. Shape the dough by pinching off pieces the size of a walnut. Roll out each piece to about 6 inches. Place 1 serving spoon of filling slightly off center on each, fold dough over filling, seal edges and fry in skillet.

Makes 6 turnovers.

# Blueberry Dump Cake

- 1 can (15 oz.) crushed PINEAPPLE
- 2 cups fresh BLUEBERRIES
- 1 pkg. (18.25 oz.) YELLOW CAKE MIX
- 2 sticks BUTTER, melted

Spray a 13 x 9 pan with nonstick spray. Layer pineapple, blueberries and dry cake mix. Do not stir. Drizzle evenly with melted butter over top. Bake at 350° for 50 minutes or until golden brown.

# Blueberries in the Snow

1/2 cup SUGAR
1/2 cup MILK
1 pkg. (8 oz.) CREAM CHEESE, softened
1 ctn. (16 oz.) WHIPPED TOPPING
1 1/2 cups fresh BLUEBERRIES
1 lg. ANGEL FOOD CAKE
1 can (21 oz.) BLUEBERRY PIE FILLING

Combine sugar, milk and cream cheese in a large bowl. Beat with electric mixer until blended. Fold in whipped topping and blueberries. Crumble angel food cake into small pieces and add to cream mixture. Mix well and pour into a large bowl, packing mixture down and spreading evenly. Pour blueberry pie filling on top and spread evenly. Cover and refrigerate for at least 3 hours before serving.

# Melt-In-Your-Mouth Blueberry Bars

1/2 cup BUTTER
3/4 cup SUGAR
2 EGGS
1 tsp. VANILLA
3/4 cup MILK
1 1/2 cups SELF-RISING FLOUR
1/2 cup ROLLED OATS
1/4 tsp. CINNAMON
1 1/2 cup fresh BLUEBERRIES, washed, drained and dusted with flour
1/4 cup packed BROWN SUGAR
1 cup POWDERED SUGAR
3-4 tsp. MILK

Cream butter and sugar. Add eggs and beat well. Stir in vanilla and milk. Mix well. Add flour, oats and cinnamon, mixing well. Add flour-coated blueberries and stir. Pour batter into a greased 9 x 9 pan. Sprinkle with brown sugar. Bake at 325° for about 30-40 minutes. Create topping by mixing powdered sugar and milk until smooth. When bars have cooled, drizzle with topping.

# Chilled Triple Berry Peach Soup

1 pt. BLUEBERRIES
1 pt. STRAWBERRIES,
　　hulled and chopped
1 cup RASPBERRIES
2 PEACHES, chopped

2 cups CRANBERRY JUICE
2 cups APPLE JUICE
1/3 cup DRY WHITE WINE
1 tsp. CINNAMON
1/4 tsp. NUTMEG

Combine all ingredients in a large soup pot. Bring to a boil, cover, reduce heat and simmer for 10-15 minutes. Cook until fruit is tender. Let cool and chill until ready to serve. Garnish with strawberry slices.

## Blueberries are Good for Your Health!

*Blueberries are referred to as "nutraceutical", which means they are a food which serves specific benefits to human health. Research has shown that certain substances in blueberries are good for your eyesight, circulation and fighting the aging process!*

# Cold Fruit Soup

2 PLUMS
1 PEAR
2 PEACHES
1/2 cup BLUEBERRIES
1/2 cup RAISINS

1 APPLE
1/2 cup APPLE JUICE
1 Tbsp. RICE SYRUP
1 frozen BANANA
1 Tbsp. CASHEW pieces

Peel, pit and prepare fruit into bite-size pieces and mix together in serving bowl. Purée apple juice, syrup and banana in a blender. Pour over fruit and top with cashews.

# Strawberries

# Strawberry
# Chicken Salad

1/2 cup MAYONNAISE
2 Tbsp. chopped CHUTNEY
1 tsp. grated LIME PEEL
1 tsp. SALT
1 tsp. CURRY POWDER
1 Tbsp. LIME JUICE

2 cups diced cooked CHICKEN
1 cup sliced CELERY
1/4 cup chopped RED ONION
1 1/2 pints fresh STRAWBERRIES
LETTUCE LEAVES

In a large bowl, combine mayonnaise, chutney, lime peel, salt, curry powder and lime juice. Add chicken, celery and onion. Toss, cover and chill. Just before serving, slice enough strawberries to make 2 cups; gently toss with chicken mixture. Line platter or individual serving plates with lettuce. Mound chicken salad in center. Garnish with remaining 1 cup whole strawberries.

*To maximize berry freshness, do not wash them right away. Layer them in a large container with a dry paper towel between layers, making sure to separate the berries. Just before using, wash strawberries with the caps attached under a gentle spray of cool water.*

# Strawberry Dressing

1/2 cup sliced, hulled STRAWBERRIES
2 Tbsp. ORANGE JUICE
2 Tbsp. RED WINE VINEGAR
1 tsp. HONEY

Purée all ingredients in a blender. Chill. Serve over fruit or green salads.

# Strawberry Preserves

**2 qt. boxes lg. firm, tart STRAWBERRIES, cleaned and hulled**
**4 1/2 cups SUGAR**

Combine whole fruit and sugar in alternate layers. Let stand for 8 to 10 hours or overnight in the refrigerator. Heat fruit mixture to boiling, stirring gently. Boil rapidly, stirring occasionally to prevent sticking. Cook to 220° or until syrup is somewhat thick (about 15 to 20 minutes). Remove from heat; skim. Process in sterilized containers according to manufacturers directions.

Makes 4 half-pints.

---

### Strawberry Measurements

*One quart of strawberries weighs 1 1/4 to 1 1/2 pounds. One cup of sliced fresh berries equals one 10-ounce package of frozen berries.*

---

# Strawberry Orange Jam

**4 cups STRAWBERRIES**        **7 cups SUGAR**
**2 ORANGES**                  **1/2 bottle LIQUID PECTIN**

Sort and wash strawberries. Remove stems and caps; crush berries. Cut unpeeled oranges into very thin wedges. Remove ends and seed as necessary. Put in saucepan, cover with water and boil 15 minutes. Drain and repeat with fresh water. Drain thoroughly and chop or dice. Combine oranges and crushed berries in a large saucepan. Add sugar and mix well. Place over high heat; bring to a full rolling boil and boil hard for one minute, stirring constantly. Remove from heat and stir in pectin immediately. Stir and skim for 5 minutes to cool slightly and prevent floating fruit. Pour into sterilized jars and seal according to manufacturer's directions.

# Strawberry Jam

**1/4 cup LEMON JUICE**
**3 qt. boxes STRAWBERRIES**

**1 pkg. POWDERED PECTIN**
**7 1/2 cups SUGAR**

Sort and wash strawberries. Remove stems and caps and crush. Place strawberries in a kettle. Add pectin and stir well. Place on high heat and, stirring constantly, bring quickly to a full boil with bubbles over the entire surface. Add sugar, continue stirring, and heat again to a full bubbling boil. Boil hard for 1 minute, stirring constantly. Remove from heat; skim.

Makes 8 cups.

### Jams & Jellies and Preserves

*Jelly is a mixture of fruit juice and sugar that is clear and firm. Jam is made from crushed or chopped fruit. Preserves are made of small, whole fruits or pieces of fruits in a clear, thick, slightly gelled syrup. Sugar helps preserve sweet spreads, contributes flavor and aids in gelling.*

# Sugarless Berry Jam

**4 cups STRAWBERRIES**
**1 pkg. POWDERED PECTIN**
**1 Tbsp. LEMON JUICE**

**3-4 tsp. LIQUID ARTIFICIAL SWEETENER**

Crush berries in saucepan. Stir in pectin and lemon juice. Bring to a boil; boil for 1 minute. Remove from heat. Stir in sweetener. For immediate use, store in a sealed container in refrigerator for up to 4 weeks. For freezing, continue to stir about 2 minutes. Pour into freezer containers, leaving 1/2-inch head space. Seal. Chill in refrigerator and store in freezer. To can, process according to manufacturer's directions.

# Champagne Wreath

2 pkgs. (6 oz. ea.) LEMON FLAVOR GELATIN
2 1/4 cups BOILING WATER
1 bottle (750 ml) chilled CHAMPAGNE
3 cups SEEDLESS GRAPES
2 cups STRAWBERRIES, sliced

Dissolve gelatin in boiling water. Add champagne and chill until partially thickened. Add fruit. Pour into a 9-cup ring mold and chill until firm. Unmold on serving platter and garnish with salad greens if desired.

Makes 8 servings.

### Picking Strawberries
*Try to pick early in the morning or on cool, cloudy days. Berries picked during the heat of the day become soft, are easily bruised, and will not keep well.*

# Strawberry Chutney

1 cup STRAWBERRY PRESERVES
1 can (17 oz.) PEAR HALVES, drained and chopped
1/4 cup RAISINS
1 Tbsp. chopped CRYSTALLIZED GINGER
1 Tbsp. LEMON JUICE
1/8 tsp. grated LEMON PEEL

Mix all ingredients in a bowl. Cover and chill at least 2 hours. Keep refrigerated to store. Excellent served with pork, chicken, turkey, duck or ham.

Makes about 2 cups.

# Summer Strawberry Salad

4 fresh PLUMS, sliced
1 cup SEEDLESS GRAPES
1 cup sliced fresh
    STRAWBERRIES
1 cup cubed CANTALOUPE

Juice of 1 LEMON
1/2 cup ORANGE JUICE
1/4 cup WHITE WINE
1/4 tsp. TARRAGON
1 BANANA, peeled and sliced

Combine first 4 ingredients in a bowl; toss lightly with lemon juice. Combine orange juice, wine and tarragon; pour over fruit and marinate 2-3 hours. Add banana just before serving.

Makes 4 servings.

### Storing and Preparing Strawberries
*Store berries uncovered in the refrigerator in the original or a shallow container. When ready to use, wash them quickly in cold water; do not soak. Drain berries well before hulling.*

# Strawberry Poppy Salad

Dressing:
    1/3 cup VEGETABLE OIL
    3 Tbsp. CIDER VINEGAR
    2 Tbsp. WATER
    1 1/2 Tbsp. HONEY

1 Tbsp. POPPY SEEDS
1/2 tsp. SALT
1/2 tsp. PAPRIKA
1/4 tsp. PEPPER

LETTUCE LEAVES
1 pint fresh STRAWBERRIES, hulled and halved
1 sm. RED ONION, sliced and separated into rings

In blender, combine oil, vinegar, water, honey, poppy seeds, salt, paprika and pepper. Blend until thoroughly mixed; set aside. Line 4 individual serving plates with lettuce. Arrange strawberries and onion rings, equally divided, on lettuce. Stir dressing before serving; pass separately.

Serves 4.

# Strawberry Fruit Salad

**Dressing:**
- 1 pt. fresh STRAWBERRIES, hulled and halved
- 1/2 tsp. DRIED MINT LEAVES
- 1/2 tsp. HONEY
- 1/2 cup LOW FAT SOUR CREAM

**RED LEAF LETTUCE**
**1 cup fresh BLUEBERRIES**
**1 cup NAVEL ORANGE slices**
**1 cup sliced STRAWBERRIES**

In a blender, purée strawberries, mint leaves, honey and sour cream. Arrange lettuce leaves on 4 serving plates. Top lettuce with blueberries, orange and strawberry slices. Pour puréed strawberry dressing over individual servings.

### Strawberries are Nutritious, Too!
*Strawberries are a good source of Vitamin C, as well as being low in calories; one cup of unsweetened strawberries has only 55 calories.*

# Strawberry Ambrosia

**1 pkg. (10 oz.) frozen sliced STRAWBERRIES, thawed**
**16 lg. MARSHMALLOWS, quartered**
**1 tsp. grated LEMON PEEL**
**2 Tbsp. LEMON JUICE**
**1 med. ORANGE, pared and diced**
**Dash of SALT**
**1 cup flaked COCONUT**
**1/2 cup HEAVY CREAM, whipped**

Combine strawberries, marshmallows, lemon peel, lemon juice, orange and salt; toss lightly. Chill 1 hour. Fold in coconut and cream.

Makes 4 servings.

# Strawberry Napoleons

**8 sheets PHYLLO DOUGH, thawed according to pkg. directions**
**3 cups PASTRY CREAM, at room temperature**
**3 cups sliced STRAWBERRIES**
**POWDERED SUGAR, for dusting**

Preheat oven to 350°. Spray a baking sheet with nonstick vegetable spray. Spray a sheet of the phyllo dough with nonstick spray, fold in half and spray again, then fold once more and spray again. Cut the folded dough in quarters to make four even rectangles. Cut each rectangle in half. Repeat the process with the remaining sheets of phyllo. Place the rectangles on the baking sheet and bake until lightly browned, 3 to 4 minutes. Watch carefully, as they burn easily. For each napoleon, spread three of the rectangles with 1 tablespoon of *Pastry Cream*, then 1 tablespoon of the berries. Stack the three layers, then top with the remaining rectangle. Lightly dust with powdered sugar. Repeat until all napoleons have been assembled.

Makes 16 napoleons.

## Pastry Cream

**3 cups LOW FAT MILK**
**2/3 cup SUGAR**
**2 WHOLE EGGS & 1 EGG YOLK**

**4 Tbsp. CORNSTARCH**
**1 1/2 Tbsp. VANILLA**

Using double boiler, heat 2 1/2 cups milk until steam rises from the surface. In a separate bowl, whisk together eggs, remaining 1/2 cup milk and sugar. Sift in cornstarch and whisk until well-blended. Remove from heat and gradually whisk in egg mixture. Return pan to top of double boiler and whisk constantly over medium heat until thickened and smooth, about 5 minutes. Remove from heat and stir in vanilla. Transfer to bowl, press plastic wrap onto pastry cream surface, and refrigerate until ready to use. Can be stored for up to 3 days.

# Strawberry Cheesecake

1 cup MILK
4 pkgs. (3 oz. ea.) CREAM CHEESE, softened
1 tsp. VANILLA
4 Tbsp. SUGAR
1 pkg. (3 oz.) LEMON INSTANT PUDDING
1 (9-inch) baked PASTRY SHELL or GRAHAM CRACKER CRUST
1 pkg. (3 oz.) STRAWBERRY GELATIN
dash of SALT
1 cup BOILING WATER
1/4 cup COLD WATER
1 pkg. (12 oz.) frozen STRAWBERRIES

Blend together milk, cream cheese, vanilla and 2 table-spoons sugar. Beat thoroughly. Add instant pudding and beat for one minute (do not overbeat). Pour into pastry shell and chill until firm. Dissolve gelatin, remaining 2 tablespoons sugar and salt in boiling water. Add cold water and frozen fruit. Stir until berries thaw and separate. Spoon over cream cheese mixture and chill until firm. Garnish with whipped cream.

**Did You Know?**
*The average person eats 3.1 pounds of fresh strawberries a year.*

# Strawberry Cheese Tarts

1 lb. LOW FAT CREAM CHEESE, softened
1/2 cup LOW FAT SOUR CREAM
3 Tbsp. SUGAR
1 tsp. grated LEMON PEEL
12 GRAHAM CRACKER TART SHELLS (3 1/2-inch size)
2/3 cup STRAWBERRY PRESERVES

Combine cream cheese, sour cream, sugar and lemon peel in small bowl; beat until smooth. Spread evenly into tart shells; refrigerate about 4 hours. Before serving, spread the straw-berry preserves evenly over the filling.

# Strawberry Pie

**Pastry:**
- 1/2 cup MARGARINE
- 1 heaping cup FLOUR
- 3 1/2 Tbsp. POWDERED SUGAR

**Filling:**
- 1 cup SUGAR
- 3 Tbsp. plus 2 tsp. CORNSTARCH
- 1 1/2 cups WATER
- 3 Tbsp. LIGHT CORN SYRUP
- 4 Tbsp. STRAWBERRY GELATIN POWDER
- 2 drops RED FOOD COLORING
- 1 qt. fresh STRAWBERRIES

Cut margarine into flour and powdered sugar. Press into a 9-inch pie pan and bake at 350° for 20 minutes; cool. Combine sugar and cornstarch in a saucepan, adding water and corn syrup. Bring to a boil and cook 6 minutes, stirring constantly. Remove from heat and add dry gelatin and red food coloring. Set aside to cool. Clean and slice the strawberries and stir into the cooled mixture. Pour into pie crust and allow to set.

# Strawberry Bread

| | |
|---|---|
| 2 Tbsp. COOKING OIL | 2 Tbsp. SUGAR |
| 12 EGGS | 18 slices STALE BREAD |
| 1 1/2 cups MILK | 1 qt. STRAWBERRIES, sliced |
| 1 tsp. CINNAMON | POWDERED SUGAR |
| 1 tsp. SALT | |

Heat oil in skillet until medium-hot. In a large bowl, mix eggs, milk, cinnamon, salt and sugar until frothy. Dip bread into mixture to cover both sides and fry until brown. Flip bread, smother with strawberries and cook until bread is brown. Top with powdered sugar and serve immediately.

# Strawberry Rhubarb Whirl

1 cup sliced STRAWBERRIES
1 cup diced RHUBARB
1 cup SUGAR
1 cup WATER
MILK
2 1/2 cups BISCUIT MIX
2 Tbsp. BUTTER or MARGARINE
HOT MAPLE SYRUP
WHIPPED STRAWBERRY TOPPING

Combine strawberries, rhubarb, sugar and water and cook for 10 minutes, stirring until sugar is dissolved. Add enough milk to biscuit mix to make rolled biscuits (follow directions on package). Roll dough into a rectangular shape about 9 x 6. Spread rhubarb and strawberries on dough. Roll up like a jellyroll, 9 inches long. Slice into six slices (1 1/2-inches thick). Lay slices flat in a baking pan. Dot with butter. Pour hot syrup over the top. Bake at 450° for 20 minutes. Serve warm with *Whipped Strawberry Topping.*

Makes 6 servings.

## Whipped Strawberry Topping

1 EGG WHITE
3 Tbsp. SUGAR
1 cup crushed STRAWBERRIES
1 tsp. LEMON JUICE

Beat egg white until foamy. Gradually beat in sugar, strawberries and lemon juice. Continue beating until stiff and fluffy.

# Strawberries & Custard

4 lg. EGGS
1/3 cup SUGAR
1/4 tsp. SALT
3 cups MILK

1 tsp. VANILLA
STRAWBERRIES, sliced
    and sweetened

Beat eggs slightly and stir in sugar and salt. Scald milk and gradually stir into egg mixture. Add vanilla and pour into six 6-ounce custard cups. Set in shallow pan and add 3/4 inch hot water. Bake at 325° for 45 minutes, or until small spatula comes out clean when inserted in center of custard. Remove from hot water, cool, then chill. Unmold and serve with fresh strawberries.

> *The strawberry was a symbol for Venus, the goddess of love, because of its natural heart shape and bright red color.*

# Strawberry Lemon Pudding

1/4 cup BUTTER
2 EGGS, separated
3 Tbsp. LEMON JUICE
1 pkg. (10 oz.) frozen sliced
    STRAWBERRIES, thawed

1 Tbsp. grated LEMON PEEL
dash of SALT
1/4 cup SUGAR
2 cups SPONGE CAKE, diced
1/2 cup chopped WALNUTS

In a saucepan, melt butter and add egg yolks, lemon juice, undrained strawberries, lemon peel and salt. Cook over low heat, stirring constantly until slightly thickened. Beat egg whites until foamy. Gradually add sugar, 1 tablespoon at a time, beating constantly until stiff and glossy. Fold egg white mixture, diced cake and walnuts into strawberry mixture. Turn into lightly buttered 1 1/2-quart baking dish. Bake at 350° for 45 minutes (or until knife inserted in center comes out clean).

# Old-Fashioned Strawberry Shortcake

**3 boxes (1 pint ea.) STRAWBERRIES**
**3/4 cup SUGAR**

**Shortcake:**
**  2 cups FLOUR**
**  1/4 cup SUGAR**
**  3 tsp. BAKING POWDER**
**  1/2 tsp. SALT**
**  1/2 cup BUTTER**
**  3/4 cup MILK**

**Topping:**
**  1 cup HEAVY CREAM**
**  2 Tbsp. POWDERED SUGAR**

Preheat oven to 450°. Wash berries in cold water, drain, remove hulls and slice into a bowl. Add sugar and mix well. Set aside until shortcake is prepared. Sift flour with sugar, baking powder and salt. Cut butter into chunks and add to flour mixture. Using pastry blender, cut butter into small particles, until coated thoroughly with flour. Make well in center of mixture and add milk. Mix quickly with fork to moisten flour, but do not overmix. (Mixture will be lumpy.) Turn into a greased 8 x 8 x 2 baking pan. Press out dough to fit corners of pan. Bake for 12 minutes (or until knife comes out clean). Loosen from pan with a sharp knife and turn out to cool on wire rack. Slit cake in half crosswise, using a serrated knife. Put bottom of cake on serving platter, cut side up. Beat heavy cream with rotary beater until stiff, and gradually stir in powdered sugar. Spoon half of the topping over bottom half of cake and layer with half of the strawberries. Place top of cake over berries and layer with remaining topping and strawberries. Garnish with whipped cream and whole or sliced strawberries.

Serves 6.

# Non-Dairy Strawberry Cream Pie

1 Tbsp. APPLE JUICE
1/2 cup VEGETABLE OIL
1 cup DATE SUGAR
1/4 cup RICE SYRUP
1/4 tsp. SEA SALT
2 (12 oz. ea.) TOFU CAKES
1 cup sliced fresh STRAWBERRIES
1 (9-inch) baked PIE CRUST
1/8 cup flaked COCONUT

Combine apple juice, oil, sugar, syrup, salt and tofu in a blender and blend until smooth and creamy. Gently fold in strawberries and pour into pie shell. Garnish with coconut flakes. Chill for 4 hours.

Serves 8.

# Strawberry Cake

1 box (18.25 oz.) MARBLE CAKE MIX
2 cans (12 oz. ea.) WHITE FROSTING
1 pt. STRAWBERRIES, sliced
1 pt. STRAWBERRIES, halved

Prepare cake mix, pour into 2 round cake pans and bake according to package directions. Cool cakes to room temperature. Remove one cake for the bottom layer. Frost with one container of frosting and place half of the sliced strawberries over the frosting. Add the second cake as the top layer. Frost with the second container of frosting and garnish the top of the cake with the remaining sliced strawberries. Place the halved strawberries on the serving plate around the bottom of the cake.

# Strawberry Cherry on a Cloud

**Meringue:**
- 6 EGG WHITES
- 1/2 tsp. CREAM OF TARTAR
- 1/4 tsp. SALT
- 1 3/4 cups SUGAR

**Filling:**
- 2 pkg. (3 oz. ea.) CREAM CHEESE, softened
- 1 cup SUGAR
- 1 tsp. VANILLA
- 2 cups WHIPPING CREAM, partially whipped and chilled
- 2 cups MINIATURE MARSHMALLOWS

**Topping:**
- 2 cups fresh STRAWBERRIES
- 1 can (21 oz.) CHERRY PIE FILLING
- 1 tsp. LEMON JUICE

Grease 13 x 9 pan. Beat egg whites, cream of tartar and salt until frothy. Gradually beat in sugar and blend until stiff and glossy, about 15 minutes. Spread in pan and bake at 275° for 90 minutes. Turn off oven and leave meringue in oven with door closed for 1 hour. Remove from oven; finish cooling away from drafts. Blend cream cheese, sugar and vanilla. Combine with chilled, partially whipped cream and beat until thick. Add marshmallows and spread over meringue. Refrigerate immediately and chill 4 hours until set. Combine ingredients for topping and spread over filling.

---

### Pick Early!
*Try to pick your berries early in the morning or on cool, cloudy days. Berries picked during the heat of the day become soft, are easily bruised and will not keep well.*

# Sweet Berry Pie

1 qt. STRAWBERRIES
1 (9-inch) DEEP DISH PIE
   SHELL, baked and cooled
1/2 cup SUGAR
1/3 cup HONEY
1/8 tsp. SALT
3 Tbsp. CORNSTARCH

1/4 cup WATER
1 tsp. BUTTER
1 cup chilled WHIPPING CREAM
1 Tbsp. POWDERED SUGAR
1/2 tsp. VANILLA
WHOLE STRAWBERRIES,
   for garnish

Rinse, pat dry and stem strawberries. Arrange 2 cups stemmed berries, hulled side down, in pie shell. Mash the remaining berries in a saucepan. Stir in sugar, honey and salt. Heat slowly, stirring often, until mixture comes to a boil. Mix cornstarch with water, then stir slowly into the boiling mixture. When thickened, remove from heat and stir in butter. Cool filling, then spread in pie shell over berries. Chill thoroughly. To make the topping; whip the cream with the powdered sugar and vanilla. Spread over pie filling and garnish with whole berries.

*Strawberries do not ripen after being picked. Also, the size of a berry does not affect its flavor.*

# Strawberry Spread

2 cups STRAWBERRIES
1/4 cup WATER
2 Tbsp. STRAWBERRY JUICE

1 1/2 tsp. ARROWROOT
   POWDER
1/4 cup BROWN RICE SYRUP

Cook strawberries in pot with water on low heat for 20 minutes. Add remaining ingredients, stirring continuously. Simmer for 20 more minutes. Chill and serve.

# Strawberry Peach Meringue Pie

**1 (9-inch) unbaked PIE CRUST**
**1/3 cup SUGAR**
**1/4 cup uncooked TAPIOCA**
**1/4 tsp. CINNAMON**
**1/4 tsp. NUTMEG**
**1/8 tsp. SALT**
**1 cup fresh sliced STRAWBERRIES**
**4 cups peeled, sliced PEACHES**

Preheat oven to 400°. In a large bowl, combine sugar, tapioca and spices. Add strawberries and peaches and mix thoroughly. Spread filling on pie crust. Bake 50-60 minutes or until golden brown. Remove pie from oven and lower heat to 350°. While pie is still hot, spread *Meringue* over filling. Bake for 12-15 minutes or until golden brown. Cool.

## Meringue

**3 lg. EGG WHITES**
   **(room temperature)**
**1/2 tsp. VANILLA**

**1/4 tsp. CREAM OF TARTAR**
**6 Tbsp. SUPERFINE SUGAR**

Beat egg whites, vanilla and cream of tartar until mixture forms stiff peaks. Add sugar gradually, 1 tablespoon at a time, beating whites until very stiff and glossy and all the sugar has dissolved.

---

### About Strawberries

*Strawberries are a small plant of the rose family. They grow close to the ground and produce small, white flowers that have a pleasant odor. The fruit is greenish white at first and then ripens to a bright red.*

---

# Strawberry Sorbet

**1 pkg. (10 oz.) frozen STRAWBERRIES in syrup**
**2 Tbsp. fresh LEMON JUICE**
**1 cup fresh ORANGE JUICE**
**3 Tbsp. ORANGE LIQUEUR**
**1 EGG WHITE**

In a blender or food processor, purée the berries with the lemon juice until very smooth. Blend in the orange juice, orange liqueur and egg white. Pour the mixture into divided ice cube trays and freeze solid. Several hours before serving, or up to a day ahead, place one third of the frozen sorbet cubes in the food processor work bowl and pulse the machine on and off until the cubes are evenly chopped to the texture of coarse snow. Then run machine continuously until the sorbet turns several shades paler and is creamy-looking. If the mixture is too hard to move freely around the bowl, allow it to melt slightly or add a few drops of water or orange juice. Process remaining cubes, or save for future use.

# Holiday Berry Punch

**1 pkg. (10 oz.) frozen STRAWBERRIES**
**1 can (12 oz.) frozen concentrated CRAN-RASPBERRY JUICE**
**1 can (12 oz.) frozen LEMONADE**
**1 ltr. GINGER ALE, chilled**
**2 ltr. SELTZER, chilled**

Thaw strawberries, place in blender with syrup and purée. Just before serving, combine strawberry purée and remaining ingredients, adding seltzer last, in a 6-quart punch bowl.

# Banana Split Float

**2 ripe med. BANANAS**
**3 cups cold MILK**
**1 1/2 pts. CHOCOLATE ICE CREAM**
**1 pkg. (10 oz.) frozen STRAWBERRIES**

In a blender, purée bananas. Add milk, 1/2 pint chocolate ice cream and strawberries; beat until just blended. Pour into tall chilled glasses and top each with a scoop of chocolate ice cream

# Strawberry Freeze

Purée 1 pint of hulled **STRAWBERRIES** in a food processor. Pour purée into small paper cups, insert a wooden stick in each and freeze.

# Frozen Strawberry Yogurt Pie

**2 ctn. (8 oz. ea.) VANILLA or STRAWBERRY FLAVORED YOGURT**
**1 ctn. (8 oz.) WHIPPED TOPPING, thawed**
**2 cups sweetened chopped STRAWBERRIES**
**1 prepared GRAHAM CRACKER CRUST**

Stir yogurt gently into whipped topping until well blended. Stir in strawberries. Spoon into crust. Freeze 4 hours or overnight until firm. Let stand in refrigerator 15 minutes or until pie can be cut easily. Garnish with additional topping and whole strawberries.

# Grilled Strawberry Kiwi Kabobs

10-12 oz. hulled fresh STRAWBERRIES
1 can (11 oz.) MANDARIN ORANGE segments, drained
1 KIWI, quartered
1 APPLE unpeeled, cored and cubed
1/2 HONEYDEW MELON or CANTALOUPE, scooped into balls
fresh wedges of PINEAPPLE

Glaze:

| | |
|---|---|
| 1 Tbsp. CORNSTARCH | 2 Tbsp. HONEY |
| juice of 1 LEMON | CINNAMON to taste |
| 1/3 cup ORANGE JUICE | 3 tsp. chopped fresh MINT |
| freshly squeezed | |

In a small saucepan, dissolve cornstarch in lemon juice. Add orange juice, honey and cinnamon. Stir until mixture thickens; add mint. Place fruit on kabob skewers, and paint fruit with glaze. Broil or grill until fruit is cooked through and lightly browned. Serve immediately.

Serves 4-6.

# Strawberry Mousse

1 1/2-2 cups crushed STRAWBERRIES (about 1 quart box)
1/4-1/2 cup SUGAR
1 Tbsp. LEMON JUICE
1 2/3 cups chilled EVAPORATED MILK

Mix together strawberries, sugar and lemon juice. Whip milk until very stiff. (Evaporated milk whips easily if it is icy cold.) Fold strawberry mixture into whipped milk. Pour immediately into cold refrigerator trays or a fancy mold and freeze.

Makes 8-10 servings.

# Sparkling Strawberry Wine Soup

**2 pint baskets fresh STRAWBERRIES, stemmed and hulled**
**1 cup DRY WINE, chilled**
**2 Tbsp. ORANGE JUICE**
**1/4 tsp. grated ORANGE RIND**
**1 cup plain SODA WATER, chilled**
**1/2 cup sliced fresh STRAWBERRIES**
**MINT LEAVES, for garnish**

Briefly purée fresh strawberries in a food processor or blender. Add chilled wine, orange juice and orange rind and blend to combine. Add soda water and stir in sliced strawberries just before serving. Garnish bowls with fresh mint leaves.

Serves 4.

---

*Strawberries are ready to harvest about 21 days after the white flowers appear.*

*For best flavor, allow strawberries to reach room temperature before serving.*

*When purchasing strawberries, choose dry, firm, fully ripe berries. The caps should be green and fresh-looking.*

---

# Strawberry Yogurt Soup

**1 1/2 cups sliced hulled STRAWBERRIES**
**2 cups NONFAT or LOW FAT PLAIN YOGURT**
**1/2 cup APPLE JUICE**
**2 Tbsp. HONEY**
**MINT SPRIGS, for garnish**

Combine all ingredients in a food processor or blender. Blend until smooth. Serve in chilled bowls. Garnish with mint.

# Strawberry Relish

1 pt. STRAWBERRIES, hulled and chopped
3 cups SEEDLESS RAISINS
1/4 cup chopped NUTS
1/2 tsp. ground GINGER
2 Tbsp. fresh LEMON JUICE
2 Tbsp. HONEY
1 Tbsp. chopped GREEN ONION

Combine all ingredients in a glass bowl and toss together. Allow to set at room temperature for 1 hour; refrigerate until serving. Excellent with poultry or fish.

### Picking Your Own Strawberries

*One of the best methods for picking straw-berries: Grasp the stem just above the berry, between the forefinger and the thumbnail and pull with a slight twisting motion. With the stem broken about one-half inch from the berry, allow it to roll into the palm of your hand. Repeat these operations using both hands until each holds 3 or 4 berries. Gently place the berries in your containers.*

# Strawberry Salsa

1 finely chopped CUCUMBER
1 thinly sliced GREEN ONION
1 Tbsp. chopped fresh CILANTRO
1 finely chopped YELLOW BELL PEPPER
3-4 Tbsp. seasoned RICE WINE VINEGAR
2 cups fresh STRAWBERRIES, hulled and diced

Mix cucumber, green onion, cilantro, bell pepper and vinegar. Cover and chill at least 1 hour. Just before serving, add strawberries. Excellent over fish.

# Raspberries

# Sweetheart Tarts

*(See cover photo)*

## Vanilla Pastry Cream

3 cups 1% MILK, divided
2/3 cup SUGAR
3 EGGS (2 whole eggs, 1 yolk)

4 Tbsp. CORNSTARCH
1 1/2 Tbsp. VANILLA

In a double boiler, heat 2 1/2 cups milk until steam rises from the surface. In a separate bowl, combine remaining 1/2 cup milk and sugar. Sift in cornstarch and whisk until well blended. Add eggs and whisk again until all is combined. Remove milk from heat and gradually whisk in egg mixture. Return pan to top of double boiler and whisk constantly over medium heat until thickened and smooth, about 5 minutes. Remove from heat and stir in vanilla. Pour into a bowl, press plastic wrap on surface and refrigerate up to 3 days.

## Red Raspberry Purée

2 cups whole frozen RASPBERRIES, thawed
2 Tbsp. BLACK RASPBERRY LIQUEUR
3-4 Tbsp. SUGAR
1 Tbsp. CORNSTARCH

Purée thawed berries in food processor or blender. Strain through a fine sieve to remove seeds. Place purée in a small saucepan. Stir sugar and cornstarch together and add to purée along with liqueur. Heat until thickened and glossy. Can be refrigerated for later use. (If purée is too cold, it may become too thick to create decorative hearts. Microwave 30-40 seconds before using.

(Continued on next page)

**Sweetheart Tarts** (Continued)

# Fruit Glaze for Tarts

**1/2 cup SEEDLESS RASPBERRY JELLY or JAM, melted**
**1 Tbsp. BLACK RASPBERRY LIQUEUR (or water)**

Combine ingredients and set aside.

# Sweetheart Pastry

*Makes 6 (4-inch) heart-shaped shells, 1-inch deep.*

**2 1/2 cups ALL-PURPOSE FLOUR, unsifted**
**4-5 Tbsp. SUGAR**
**1/2 tsp. SALT**
**2 sticks BUTTER, well-chilled**
**about 4 Tbsp. ORANGE JUICE (or water)**

Combine flour, sugar and salt in a mixing bowl; stir to blend. Slice each butter cube into 7-8 pieces. Using pastry blender or two knives, cut butter into flour mixture until all resembles coarse meal. Add orange juice (or water) by tablespoons, mixing gently with a fork just until dough begins to hold together in clumps. Gather pastry and divide evenly into six disks. Wrap each disk in plastic and chill for 30 minutes.

On lightly floured wax paper, roll each disk into a circle at least 6-inches in diameter and slightly less than 1/8-inch thick. Transfer to tart pans and gently press dough into each one, being careful not to stretch pastry. Trim the overhanging pastry dough by rolling over edges with a rolling pin, creating a finished look. Pierce the bottoms with a fork, place on a rimmed baking sheet and freeze at least 30 minutes.*

Pre-heat oven to 375°. Transfer tarts to another rimmed baking sheet which is at room temperature. Line tarts with a lightweight aluminum foil or crumpled parchment and fill with beans, rice or other pie weights. Bake while still frozen on the lowest oven rack for 15 minutes. Carefully remove weights and

(Continued on next page)

**Sweetheart Tarts** (Continued)

liner. Return tarts to oven and bake approximately 15 minutes more, until deep golden brown. Cool on wire rack.

*If wrapped well, pastry may be frozen for up to 2 months.

# Chocolate Pastry

For light chocolate pastry, replace 1/4 cup of flour with 1/4 cup of cocoa and use the higher amount of sugar. For darker chocolate crusts, replace 1/2 cup of flour with 1/2 cup of cocoa and use the higher amount of sugar.

# Raspberry, Blackberry Tarts

Begin assembly 1-2 hours before serving time. Each heart-shaped tart will require approximately 1 cup frozen raspberries or blackberries. Combinations might include half raspberry and half blackberry.

Spoon 3-4 tablespoons pastry cream into each pastry shell. Arrange evenly shaped frozen berries, stem-side down, over the pastry cream, starting around the outside edge and working towards the center. Raspberries should be arranged in two layers, while blackberries may be arranged in a single layer due to their larger size. Refrigerate until ready to serve. Just prior to serving, spoon glaze generously over berries. Garnish with your choice of orange zest, fresh mint or kiwi slices.

# Red Raspberry Purée or Vanilla Cream Tarts

Spoon 5-6 tablespoons purée into each pastry shell. Make decorative hearts by running a toothpick through droplets of vanilla cream you have strategically placed on purée surface. For vanilla cream tartlets, reverse this process, using red raspberry puree droplets on surface of the vanilla cream. Chill until serving time.

# Peach Sorbet
# with
# Red Raspberry Melba Sauce

**Sorbet:**
  1 can (29 oz.) PEACHES
  1 cup SUGAR
  1/3 cup LIGHT CORN SYRUP
  1 cup WATER
  1/4 cup fresh LEMON JUICE
**Sauce:**
  1 pkg. (12 oz.) whole frozen RASPBERRIES, thawed
  1 Tbsp. RASPBERRY LIQUEUR
  1/3 cup SUGAR

**3 cups fresh RASPBERRIES or 12 oz. frozen, partially thawed**

Drain peaches, reserving 1 cup juice. Combine reserved juice, 1 cup sugar, and corn syrup in a small saucepan. Bring to a boil, stirring constantly until all sugar is dissolved. Reduce heat and simmer for 3 minutes. Cool to room temperature. Process drained peaches in blender and blend until smooth, about 10 seconds. Add lemon juice, water and syrup mixture. Process another 10 seconds, or until contents are combined. Pour into an 8 x 8 pan and freeze for 4 hours, or until firm enough to scoop. To make sauce, purée raspberries and blend in blender for 10 seconds, or until smooth. Strain if desired, to remove seeds. Stir in liqueur and 1/3 cup sugar. Refrigerate until ready to serve. To serve, scoop and layer sorbet, raspberry melba sauce and fresh raspberries in tall parfait glasses, starting with a layer of sauce on the bottom.

Serves 6.

*Raspberries, blackberries, boysenberries and marionberries are known as caneberries, as they grow on leafy canes.*

# Raspberry Plum Butter

2 lbs. fresh PLUMS, quartered
1 pkg. (10 oz.) frozen RASPBERRIES, thawed
1 cup WATER
2 1/2 cups SUGAR
2 Tbsp. LEMON JUICE

Combine plums, thawed raspberries, with liquids and water in a heavy kettle. Bring to a boil, reduce heat and cook until fruit is very tender. Remove from heat and purée in blender. Return purée to kettle and add remaining ingredients. Cook over low heat until sugar is dissolved. Increase heat and, stirring constantly, cook until butter is thick and glossy. (Butter is ready for canning when it sheets from a spoon. Another test for butter consistency is to drop a spoonful onto a plate—if no rim of liquid forms around the edge of the butter, it's ready to be poured into sterilized jars.) Seal according to manufacturer's directions.

Makes 2 pints.

# Pear Raspberry Jam

6 or 7 RIPE PEARS
1 pkg. (10 oz.) frozen
   RASPBERRIES, thawed
1/2 cup LEMON JUICE
6 cups SUGAR
1/2 bottle FRUIT PECTIN

Peel and finely chop pears. Measure raspberries and add pears to make 4 cups. Place in a large pan, add lemon juice and sugar. Mix well; place over high heat. Bring to a full rolling boil; boil hard for one minute, stirring constantly. Remove from heat and quickly stir in pectin; skim off foam. Stir and skim for about 5 minutes. Ladle quickly into sterilized glass containers. Seal according to manufacturer's directions.

Fills about 10 medium glass jars.

# Raspberry Dream Bars

1 1/4 cups FLOUR
1 1/2 tsp. BAKING POWDER
1/2 tsp. SALT
1/4 cup BUTTER, softened
1 1/2 cups firmly packed
    BROWN SUGAR
1 Tbsp. LEMON JUICE

1 can (16.5 oz.) RASPBERRIES
2 EGGS, beaten
1/4 cup FLOUR
1 tsp. VANILLA
1 cup flaked COCONUT
3/4 cup chopped NUTS

Sift together 1 1/4 cups flour, baking powder and salt. Cream together butter and 1/2 cup brown sugar until light and fluffy. Stir in lemon juice. Cut in flour mixture until mixture resembles coarse crumbs. Press firmly in bottom of an ungreased 9 x 9 inch baking pan. Bake in a 350° oven for 15-20 minutes or until lightly browned. Cool cookie layer in pan on wire rack for 5 minutes. Spread raspberries evenly over cookie layer. Blend together eggs, 1 cup brown sugar, 1/4 cup flour and vanilla. Stir in coconut and nuts. Spread coconut mixture over raspberries. Return to oven and bake 30-35 minutes longer, or until golden brown. Cool in pan on wire rack for 5 minutes, then cut into small rectangular bars. Cool 30 minutes longer before removing from pan.

# Raspberry Pie Supreme

4-5 cups RASPBERRIES
1 (9-inch) unbaked PIE CRUST
1 1/4-1 1/2 cups SUGAR
1 cup FLOUR

1/4 tsp. SALT
1 cup SOUR CREAM
2 tsp. SUGAR

Spread raspberries on bottom of pie shell; set aside. In mixing bowl, combine sugar, flour and salt. Stir in sour cream and mix well. Spoon this mixture over berries, spreading to edges of pie crust. Sprinkle with remaining sugar and bake at 450° for 10 minutes. Reduce heat to 350° and bake for another 30 minutes or until top is lightly browned.

# Raspberries & Cream Pineapple Salad

1 pkg. (3 oz.) LEMON GELATIN
2 cups BOILING WATER
4 cups MINIATURE MARSHMALLOWS
1 pkg. (3 oz.) RASPBERRY GELATIN
1 1/3 cups BOILING WATER
1 pkg. (10 oz.) frozen RASPBERRIES
1 pkg. (8 oz.) CREAM CHEESE, softened
1 cup HEAVY CREAM
1 can (8 oz.) crushed PINEAPPLE, undrained

In a large bowl, stir lemon gelatin into boiling water until gelatin is completely dissolved. Stir in marshmallows and set aside. In a medium bowl, stir raspberry gelatin and boiling water until completely dissolved. Add frozen raspberries; stir until thawed. Pour into an 8-cup mold. Refrigerate until set but not firm, about 20-30 minutes. In a small bowl, using a mixer at medium speed, beat cream cheese until smooth. Gradually beat in heavy cream; continue beating until thick and fluffy. Set aside. Place bowl of lemon gelatin in a large bowl of ice cubes and water. Stir until gelatin mixture is slightly thickened; stir in undrained pineapple. Fold in cream cheese mixture; spoon over raspberry layer and cover. Refrigerate until firm; unmold onto serving plate.

Serves 16.

## Antioxidantally

*Antioxidant characteristics in berries appear to be due largely to the fruit's anthocyanin content. Anthocyanins are compounds acting as pigment that provide color to the berries.*

# Easy Fruit Medley

3/4 cup SUGAR
1/4 cup LIGHT CORN SYRUP
2 cups WATER
2 Tbsp. ORANGE JUICE CONCENTRATE
2 Tbsp. LEMONADE CONCENTRATE
1/4 WATERMELON
1/2 CANTALOUPE
1/2 HONEYDEW MELON
3/4 lb. RED and GREEN GRAPES, whole
3/4 lb. PEACHES, sliced
2 cups whole frozen BLACKBERRIES
2 cups whole frozen RASPBERRIES

Heat sugar, corn syrup and water until sugar is dissolved. Remove from heat and add juice concentrates. Set aside to cool. Slice and seed all melons. Cut into bite-sized pieces, or use a melon baller if desired. Add whole grapes and sliced peaches. Add frozen berries last, pouring flavored syrup over all. Place berries in 1-quart freezer bags and freeze until ready to use. (Do not freeze in larger quantities, as they will not thaw properly.) Remove from freezer about thirty minutes before serving time. Fruit should be slushy when served.

# Raspberry Loaves

1/2 cup BUTTER, softened
1/2 cup SUGAR
2 EGGS
1/3 cup SOUR CREAM
2 cups FLOUR

1 tsp. BAKING POWDER
1/2 tsp. BAKING SODA
1/2 tsp. SALT
1 cup RASPBERRIES
1/2 cup chopped NUTS

Cream butter and sugar together. Add eggs and beat until fluffy. Add sour cream and stir. In another bowl, mix flour, baking powder, baking soda and salt. Combine both mixtures, then gently fold in raspberries and nuts. Spoon dough into 2 greased 8 x 4 loaf pans. Bake at 350° for 40-50 minutes.

# Raspberry Sticky Rolls

1 loaf (16 oz.) frozen BREAD DOUGH, thawed
2 Tbsp. BUTTER, softened
1 cup BROWN SUGAR
1 can (16.5 oz.) RASPBERRIES, drained and juice reserved

Preheat oven to 375°. On lightly floured surface, roll dough into 15 x 9-inch rectangle. Spread butter over entire surface and sprinkle with brown sugar and raspberries. Beginning on 15-inch side, roll up tightly, jellyroll style. Pinch edge of dough into roll to seal well. Stretch roll to make even. Cut into 15 equal pieces. Place 3 across and 5 down over **Raspberry Topping,** keeping rolls slightly apart. Let rise until double, about 35-45 minutes. Bake until golden brown, 25-30 minutes. Remove from oven and immediately invert pan on a heatproof platter. Let pan remain a minute or two so raspberry topping can drizzle over rolls.

Makes 15 servings.

## Raspberry Topping

1/2 cup SUGAR
2 Tbsp. CORNSTARCH

reserved RASPBERRY
JUICE

In a small saucepan mix together sugar and cornstarch. Gradually add reserved raspberry juice. Cook and stir over medium heat until thickened. Set aside to cool, then pour into a greased 15 x 10 pan.

### About Raspberries

*Each berry looks like a cluster of tiny beads, colored red, black, or purple. The beads are called drupelets. Each drupelet contains a tiny seed. This thorny bush belongs to the rose family.*

# Raspberry Lemon Streusel Muffins

2 1/2 cups FLOUR
2 tsp. BAKING POWDER
1 tsp. BAKING SODA
1 1/3 cups SUGAR
1 Tbsp. grated LEMON PEEL
1 EGG

1 cup BUTTERMILK
1/2 cup melted BUTTER
1 Tbsp. LEMON JUICE
1 1/2 cups whole frozen
    RASPBERRIES
1 Tbsp. FLOUR

In a large mixing bowl, combine flour, baking powder, baking soda, sugar and lemon peel. In a separate bowl, combine egg, buttermilk, butter and lemon juice. Add to dry ingredients and stir until almost fully mixed. Toss frozen raspberries with flour to coat, then gently fold into dough. Place paper muffin liners in muffin tin, and fill each to 3/4 full. Crumble **Lemon Streusel Topping** over each. Bake for 15 minutes; reduce heat to 350°; bake for another 10 minutes, or until lightly browned.

## Lemon Streusel Topping

1/4 cup melted BUTTER
1/2 cup FLOUR

2 Tbsp. SUGAR
1 1/2 tsp. grated LEMON PEEL

Mix together topping ingredients and set aside.

# Raspberry Cranberry Ring

1 pkg. (3 oz.) RASPBERRY GELATIN
1 pkg. (3 oz.) LEMON GELATIN
2 cups BOILING WATER
1 pkg. (10 oz.) frozen RASPBERRIES
1 cup CRANBERRY-ORANGE RELISH
7 oz. bottled LEMON LIME carbonated beverage

Dissolve gelatins in boiling water. Stir in raspberries and relish. Chill until cold but not set. Resting bottle on rim of bowl, pour in beverage. Stir gently with up and down motion. Pour into ring mold. Chill until firm.

# Raspberry Shake

**1 cup VANILLA ICE CREAM**          **1 cup GINGER ALE**
**3/4 cup fresh RASPBERRIES**

Combine vanilla ice cream and raspberries in blender. Blend until smooth. Add ginger ale, blend briefly, until desired consistency is achieved.

# Citrus Berry Mimosas

**6 oz. frozen ORANGE JUICE CONCENTRATE**
**6 oz. frozen PINEAPPLE JUICE CONCENTRATE**
**2 cups RASPBERRY JUICE**
**1 can (12 oz.) LEMON-LIME SODA, chilled**
**ORANGE SLICES**
**RASPBERRIES**

In a punch bowl, combine juices. Just before serving, add soda, orange slices and raspberries.

# Sparkling
# Berry Champagne

**1 btl. (750 ml) CHAMPAGNE, chilled**
**1 cup RED RASPBERRY JUICE**
**1/4 cup BLACK RASPBERRY LIQUEUR**
**Fresh or frozen whole RASPBERRIES, for garnish**
**Fresh MINT, for garnish**

Divide juice and liqueur evenly between 4 wine glasses. Fill glasses with champagne, adding 2-3 raspberries and sprig of fresh mint for garnish.

# Blackberries

# Blackberry Summer Salad

1 can (16.5 oz.) BLACKBERRIES
2 med. NECTARINES or PEACHES, pared or sliced
2 med. KIWI FRUIT, pared and sliced, or 6 PINEAPPLE SPEARS
1/2 med. CANTALOUPE or HONEYDEW MELON, cut into spears
2 med. BANANAS, peeled and sliced
6 LETTUCE LEAVES

Drain blackberries, reserving syrup for dressing. Arrange fruit on lettuce-lined salad plates. Serve **Blackberry Yogurt Dressing** with salad.

## Blackberry Yogurt Dressing

Stir **1/4 cup reserved BLACKBERRY SYRUP, 1 tablespoon HONEY** and **2 teaspoons chopped MINT** into **1 carton (8 oz.) LOW FAT PLAIN YOGURT**.

Makes about 1 cup.

*When picking blackberries, pick only ripe berries, these are black all over with no red drupelets. Handle blackberries gently! You do not need to wash blackberries prior to storing in the refrigerator or freezer.*

*Blackberries and raspberries are high in vitamins A and C, calcium and iron. They are fat-free foods which are also high in fiber. Caneberries are recognized as being nutraceuticals, as they are foods which provide medical or health benefits.*

*Blackberries and raspberries have a high content of ellagic acid, a naturally occurring organic acid that, according to medical studies, inhibits the initiation of cancer cells induced by certain chemicals.*

# Crab Won Tons
## with
# Blackberry Szechuan Sauce

**Blackberry Szechuan Sauce:**
- 1/2 cup BLACKBERRY PURÉE
- 1/2 cup SAKI or DRY SHERRY
- 1 Tbsp. CORNSTARCH
- 1/2 tsp. SALT
- 1/2 tsp. RED PEPPER FLAKES
- 1/2 tsp. grated GINGER
- 1 tsp. LIME JUICE
- 2 cloves, GARLIC minced
- 1 1/2 Tbsp. HONEY

**Filling:**
- 2-3 oz. fresh SPINACH, trimmed and washed
- 1 Tbsp. BUTTER
- 4 Tbsp. finely chopped ONION
- 3 oz. CREAM CHEESE, cut into small chunks
- 2 Tbsp. LEMON JUICE
- SALT and PEPPER to taste
- TABASCO® (optional)
- 1/2 lb. flaked, cooked CRABMEAT
- 2 Tbsp. dry BREADCRUMBS
- 3 doz. WON TON WRAPPERS
- VEGETABLE OIL

Mix sauce ingredients in saucepan. Bring to a boil over medium high heat and cook until clear and thickened. (The flavor of this sauce improves after standing overnight.) To prepare the filling, begin by washing the spinach. With water still clinging to the leaves, place the spinach in a large pan over medium high heat. Cook until spinach begins to wilt and most of the water has evaporated. Empty onto cutting board and

(Continued on next page)

**Crab Won Tons with Blackberry Szechuan Sauce**
(Continued)

finely chop. Set aside. Melt butter in sauté pan. Add onion and sauté until translucent. Reduce heat to low; add cream cheese. When cream cheese begins to soften, blend in lemon juice, salt, pepper and Tabasco. Remove from heat and stir in crab, spinach and breadcrumbs. To prepare won tons, place 1-2 teaspoons filling in each wrapper and seal according to package directions. Place single layer of won tons in hot oil and fry 2-3 minutes until golden brown. Drain on paper towels and serve immediately with *Blackberry Szechuan Sauce.*

> *Marionberries,* native to Oregon, are a very
> flavorful variety of blackberry.

# Cornish Game Hens with Wild Blackberry Sauce

| | |
|---|---|
| 4 whole **CORNISH GAME HENS** | 1/8 tsp. **CINNAMON** |
| 1/4 tsp. **CUMIN** | 1 cup **BLACKBERRIES** |
| 1/4 tsp. **OREGANO** | 1/4 cup **SHERRY** |
| 1/4 tsp. **THYME** | 1/4 cup **SOY SAUCE** |
| 1/2 tsp. **GARLIC POWDER** | 1 tsp. **GARLIC POWDER** |
| 1/2 tsp. **PEPPER** | 1 cup **WATER** |
| 1 tsp. **SALT** | |

Season hens by rubbing mixture of spices on skin. Roast on rack in pan at 350° for 30 minutes. Combine berries, sherry, soy sauce and garlic powder and baste hens. Add water to the pan; cover hens with oiled foil or pan cover. Bake 45 minutes to one hour; drain liquid. Reduce hen juices; baste again before serving. Serve with pan juices over rice.

# Blackberry Fruit Tart

**Crust;**
    1 1/2 cups ALL-PURPOSE FLOUR
    1/2 cup SUGAR
    1/2 cup BUTTER, cut into 1-inch pieces
    1 EGG, slightly beaten
    1 EGG WHITE

**Filling:**
    12 oz. LOW FAT CREAM CHEESE
    1/3 cup SOUR CREAM
    1/2 cup SUGAR
    1 1/2 tsp. grated ORANGE PEEL
    3 Tbsp. ORANGE JUICE

**Purée:**
    2 cups fresh or whole frozen BLACKBERRIES, thawed
    6 Tbsp. SUGAR
    1 1/2 Tbsp. CORNSTARCH
    1 1/2 Tbsp. COLD WATER

**Garnish:**
    3 cups fresh or whole frozen BLACKBERRIES, partially thawed
        and drained

In a large mixing bowl, combine flour, sugar and butter. Beat at medium speed, scraping bowl often until mixture is crumbly (approximately 2-3 minutes). (If using food processor, combine same ingredients in processor bowl, making sure butter is cold. Pulse 10-15 times. Remove to mixer bowl.) Make well in center of flour mixture and pour in egg, reserving egg white for later. Blend with fork until incorporated thoroughly. Mixture will be very dry. Press dough out to 1/4-inch thickness on bottom and sides of 10-inch tart pan with removable bottom. Chill for 1 hour. Heat oven to 400°. Brush crust with beaten egg white and bake 15 to 20 minutes or until golden brown. Cool. Beat together softened cream cheese with sour cream. Add

(Continued on next page)

**Blackberry Fruit Tart** (Continued)

sugar, grated peel and juice and beat until smooth. Spread evenly over prepared crust and refrigerate. Place berries in processor bowl and process until puréed. Place in saucepan and cook on medium heat 2 to 3 minutes. Add sugar and continue to cook another 5 minutes. Combine cornstarch and cold water. Gradually add cornstarch mixture to berry mixture to thicken. Cool. Pour cooled purée over filling. Just before serving, garnish by placing fresh or partially thawed individual berries over top. Refrigerate until serving.

Serves 8-10.

# Blackberry Breakfast Bars

16 oz. fresh, frozen or canned
   BLACKBERRIES
2 1/2 Tbsp. CORNSTARCH
1 Tbsp. LEMON JUICE
1 cup ALL-PURPOSE FLOUR
1 cup WHOLE-WHEAT FLOUR
2 cups QUICK OATS
1 cup packed BROWN SUGAR
1 1/4 tsp. BAKING POWDER
3/4 tsp. SALT
1/2 tsp. ground ALLSPICE
1 tsp. CINNAMON
1 cup BUTTER

Preheat oven to 400°. Thaw berries if frozen. Warm berries in saucepan until the juices run. (If using canned berries, omit this step and simply drain berries from can, reserving juices.) Measure juices, adding water if necessary to make one cup. Combine cooled reserved juice with cornstarch and lemon juice in a saucepan. Cook and stir until thickened. Gently stir in blackberries. Set aside. Combine flours, oats, brown sugar, baking powder, salt and spices. Cut in butter until crumbly. Press 2/3 of mixture into greased 13 x 9 pan. Bake 15 minutes or until browned. Cool slightly; spread blackberries over this crust. Crumble remaining flour/oat mixture over berry layer and press lightly. Bake 20-25 minutes more, until lightly browned. Cool in pan.

# Blackberry Cheesecake

**Blackberry Sauce:**
    1 can (16.5 oz.) BLACKBERRIES
    3 tsp. CORNSTARCH

**Cheesecake**
    VEGETABLE COOKING SPRAY
    1/3 cup VANILLA WAFER CRUMBS
    1 cup LOW FAT COTTAGE CHEESE
    3 pkg. (8 oz. ea.) LOW FAT CREAM CHEESE, softened
    1 1/2 cups SUGAR, divided
    2 EGGS
    2-3 tsp. VANILLA
    2 EGG WHITES
    1/8 tsp. CREAM OF TARTAR
    1 cup NON FAT SOUR CREAM

Combine 1/2 cup blackberries and syrup and 1 teaspoon cornstarch; mix well and cook until thickened. Purée and set aside. Drain remaining blackberries and syrup; reserve both. Add remaining cornstarch to syrup and cook until thickened; add drained blackberries to thickened syrup and set aside. Coat bottom of a 9-inch pan with cooking spray; sprinkle vanilla wafer crumbs evenly over bottom of pan. Process cottage cheese in food processor or blender until smooth and creamy. In large mixing bowl, beat cream cheese, 1 cup sugar, whole eggs and vanilla until smooth; beat in cottage cheese. In small mixing bowl, beat egg whites and cream of tartar until foamy; gradually add 1/4 cup sugar and beat until stiff peaks form and sugar dissolves. Fold egg white mixture into cheese mixture. Spoon mixture into pan. Bake at 325° for 50 minutes or until almost set. Remove from oven and raise temperature to 375°. Combine sour cream and remaining sugar; mix to blend. Spread mixture over top of cheesecake. Drizzle 1/2 cup thickened blackberry purée mixture over top of sour cream; let set for 5 minutes, cool on wire rack. Cover and refrigerate until completely chilled. Serve on or with *Blackberry Sauce.*

# Quick Blackberry Cobbler

1 cup FLOUR
1 cup SUGAR
1 tsp. BAKING POWDER
1/2 tsp. SALT
2 pints BLACKBERRIES
1 stick BUTTER

3/4 cup MILK
1/2 cup SUGAR
CINNAMON and/or
      NUTMEG (optional)

Preheat oven to 350°. Sift together dry ingredients. Melt butter, in oven, in a 13 x 9 pan. When melted, pour in dry ingredients and milk to make batter. Distribute evenly. Do not stir. Distribute 1/2 cup sugar on top. Sprinkle cinnamon or nutmeg as desired. Bake about 30 minutes or until done. Puncture crust with toothpick to determine when done.

# Blackberry Mousse

1 can (16.5 oz.) BLACKBERRIES
WATER
1/4 cup SUGAR
1 env. GELATIN
1 EGG WHITE, stiffly beaten
1 cup HEAVY CREAM, whipped
1 Tbsp. ORANGE LIQUEUR

Drain blackberries; reserve syrup. Reserve 6 blackberries for garnish. Add water to reserved syrup to equal 1 cup. Heat blackberries, syrup mixture and sugar. Soften gelatin in 1/4 cup water; stir into blackberry mixture to dissolve. Chill until mixture is partially thickened. Fold in beaten egg white; whipped cream and liqueur. Chill until nearly set. Spoon into 6 stemmed goblets. Garnish with reserved blackberries. Refrigerate until served.

Makes 6 servings.

# Wild Blackberry Pie

**Crust:**

2 cups FLOUR          1 tsp. SALT
2/3 cup SHORTENING

**Filling:**

4 cups WILD BLACKBERRIES     1/4 cup FLOUR
3/4 cup SUGAR               NUTMEG to taste
1 tsp. CINNAMON

Blend crust ingredients with pastry blender. In small bowl, place 1 cup pastry mix, add 2 1/2 tablespoons ice water and mix. Form into ball and roll out with rolling pin. Fold in half and place in 8-inch pie dish. Trim edge to 1/2 inch of pie dish. Pour filling into crust. Take additional cup of pie crust mix, and combine with another 2 1/2 tablespoons of ice water. Form into ball and roll out to a size that will fit the pie. Cut rolled out dough into strips and weave on top of pie. Trim edge to 1/2 inch over pie dish. Fold under with bottom crust. Using thumb and index fingers, make a fluted edge. Bake at 375° for one hour. Let cool for 2 or 3 hours.

Note: For a sweeter pie, use 1 cup of sugar.

# Blackberry Cake

2 cups SUGAR              3 tsp. CINNAMON
1 cup BUTTER             3 tsp. ALLSPICE
4 EGGS                   1 tsp. NUTMEG
1 tsp. BAKING SODA       1 cup BUTTERMILK
1 tsp. BAKING POWDER     1 1/2 cups BLACKBERRY
3 1/2 cups CAKE FLOUR        JAM or PRESERVES

Thoroughly cream sugar, butter and eggs. Sift all dry ingredients together 3 times. Add alternately with buttermilk to creamed mixture. Add jam and mix thoroughly. Pour batter into 2-4 greased and floured layer pans. Bake at 350° 20-25 minutes. Put together with your favorite vanilla icing.

# Blackberry Peach Crisp

**1 cup ROLLED OATS**
**1 cup packed BROWN SUGAR**
**3/4 cup FLOUR**
**1/2 cup BUTTER**
**4 cups BLACKBERRIES**
**2 cups sliced PEACHES**

Preheat oven to 350°. Combine oats, brown sugar and 1/2 cup flour. Cut in butter with pastry blender or two knives until well-blended and moist enough to form a ball. Place well-drained berries in bottom of 8 x 8 baking dish and toss with remaining 1/4 cup flour. Add well-drained peaches to baking dish. Sprinkle crumb mixture evenly over fruit and bake for 35-40 minutes or until golden brown.

# Banana Blackberry Surprise

**2 ripe BANANAS**
**1 cup BLACKBERRIES**

**1 tsp. BROWN RICE SYRUP**
**3 Tbsp. CASHEW pieces**

Slice bananas into 1/4-inch slices. In bowl, mix bananas and blackberries. Mix in brown rice syrup. Top with cashew pieces.

# Blackberry Malted

**1 cup fresh BLACKBERRIES**
**1 frozen BANANA**

**2 cups SOY MILK**
**1 tsp. SORGHUM**

Combine all ingredients in blender and blend until smooth.

Yields 2 glasses.

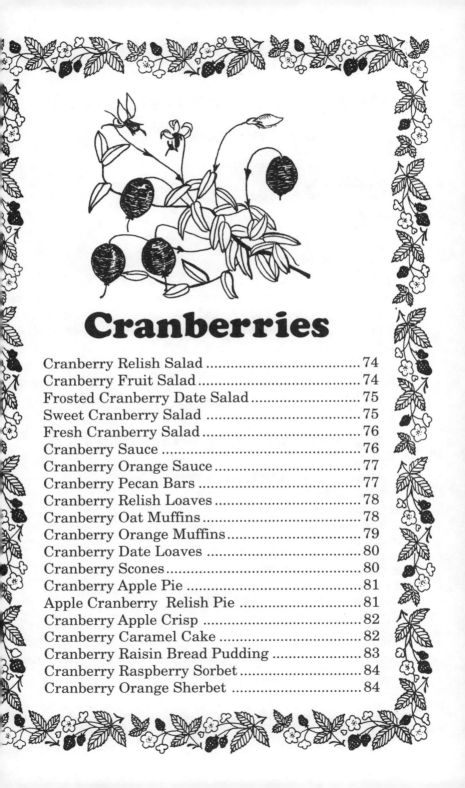

# Cranberries

# Cranberry Relish Salad

1 pkg. (3 oz.) STRAWBERRY GELATIN
3/4 cup BOILING WATER
1 can (8 oz.) crushed PINEAPPLE
1 Tbsp. LEMON JUICE
1 cup chopped CRANBERRIES
1 Tbsp. SUGAR
dash of SALT
1/2 cup diced CELERY
1/4 cup chopped NUTS
MAYONNAISE

Dissolve gelatin in boiling water. Drain pineapple and add enough water to pineapple liquid to make 3/4 cup. Add pineapple juice and lemon juice to gelatin. Chill until thickened. In a bowl, toss together cranberries, sugar and salt. Add crushed pineapple, celery and nuts. Stir in gelatin. Place mixture in a casserole dish or individual molds. When serving, top each with a dollop of mayonnaise.

# Cranberry Fruit Salad

1 pkg. (6 oz.) STRAWBERRY GELATIN
1/2 cup BOILING WATER
1 can (16 oz.) WHOLE CRANBERRY SAUCE
1 1/2 cups GINGER ALE
1 cup chopped NUTS
1 cup chopped unpeeled APPLES
1 can (8 oz.) crushed PINEAPPLE, drained
1 BANANA, diced
1 pkg. (3 oz.) CREAM CHEESE, softened

Dissolve gelatin in boiling water. Add cranberry sauce and ginger ale. Cool until mixture begins to thicken. Add nuts, apples, pineapple and banana. Pour into 9 x 9 pan. Chill until firm, then top with softened cream cheese.

# Frosted
# Cranberry Date Salad

1 cup finely chopped
    CRANBERRIES
1/3 cup SUGAR
2 med. ORANGES
1 tsp. VANILLA
1 pkg. (8 oz.) CREAM CHEESE, softened

1 sm. APPLE, finely chopped
1/2 cup pitted WHOLE DATES
1 cup WHIPPING CREAM
LEAF LETTUCE

Combine cranberries and sugar; let stand 10 minutes. Peel and section one of the oranges. Chop orange sections, reserving juice. Squeeze remaining orange to make 1/3 cup juice, adding reserved juice if necessary. Gradually beat orange juice and vanilla into cream cheese. Stir in cranberry mixture, chopped orange sections, apple and dates. Whip cream until soft peaks form. Fold into cream cheese mixture. Spoon into an 8 x 4 x 2 loaf pan and cover and freeze until firm. To serve, let stand at room temperature for 15-20 minutes to thaw slightly. Unmold and serve on lettuce-lined plates.

# Sweet Cranberry Salad

1 lb. CRANBERRIES, ground
1 cup SUGAR
1 can (20 oz.) crushed PINEAPPLE
1 lb. MARSHMALLOWS, cut into quarters
1 pt. WHIPPING CREAM

In a bowl, mix cranberries and sugar together; set aside. In another bowl, combine crushed pineapple and marshmallows together. Let both mixtures sit overnight in the refrigerator. The next day, combine the mixtures, mixing well. Whip the cream and combine with fruit mixture.

Note: You will find that cranberries are easier to grind if you freeze them first!

# Fresh Cranberry Salad

1 pkg. (6 oz.) STRAWBERRY GELATIN
2 cups BOILING WATER
1 tsp. grated ORANGE PEEL
1 can (20 oz.) crushed PINEAPPLE, drained, juice reserved
2 Tbsp. LEMON JUICE
1 cup fresh chopped CRANBERRIES
1/2 cup diced CELERY
2/3 cup chopped WALNUTS
LETTUCE LEAVES

Dissolve gelatin in water. Stir in orange peel. Pour reserved pineapple juice into 2-cup measure. Add lemon juice and enough cold water to total 2 cups. Stir into gelatin mixture. Refrigerate 60-90 minutes, until mixture begins to thicken. Fold in cranberries, celery, walnuts and pineapple. Pour into lightly oiled 2-quart mold. Chill at least 24 hours. Line round platter with lettuce leaves. Loosen edge of mold with thin knife. Dip mold quickly in hot water to loosen and invert salad onto lettuce leaves.

*Cranberries can be refrigerated, tightly wrapped, for at least 2 months, or frozen for up to a year.*

# Cranberry Sauce

1 NAVEL ORANGE
1 1/2 cups SUGAR
1/2 tsp. grated GINGER

4 cups CRANBERRIES
1/2 cup chopped toasted
    PECANS

Grate the orange peel and add to a pot with the sugar and ginger. Add the juice from the orange to the pot and simmer over medium heat until the sugar is dissolved. Add the cranberries and cook until they pop, about 5 minutes. Add pecans and cool.

# Cranberry Orange Sauce

2 cups SUGAR
1 1/2 cups WATER
24 oz. fresh CRANBERRIES
1/2 cup DRY WHITE WINE
1 ORANGE (juice and grated peel)
1 stick CINNAMON

In a saucepan, add sugar and water and bring to a boil. Add the cranberries and remaining ingredients. Bring to a boil, then lower heat and cook for 15-20 minutes. Remove the cinnamon stick and strain the mixture, reserving the liquid. Place the ingredients from the sieve into a food processor and process for one minute. Pour this mixture and the reserved liquid into a saucepan along with the cinnamon stick and simmer for 15 more minutes to thicken.

# Cranberry Pecan Bars

1/4 cup BUTTER
1 cup FLOUR
1/2 cup packed BROWN
    SUGAR
1 tsp. finely grated ORANGE
    PEEL
1/2 cup ORANGE JUICE
1 EGG
1/2 tsp. BAKING POWDER
1/4 tsp. BAKING SODA
1/2 cup chopped PECANS
1/2 cup chopped CRANBERRIES
POWDERED SUGAR

In a mixing bowl, beat butter with electric mixer on medium speed for 30 seconds. Add about 1/2 cup flour, brown sugar, orange peel, 1/4 cup orange juice, egg, baking powder and baking soda. Beat until thoroughly combined. Beat in remaining flour and orange juice. Stir in pecans and cranberries. Spread into an ungreased 11 x 7 baking pan. Bake at 350° for about 25 minutes. Cool in the pan on a wire rack. Sift powdered sugar over the top. Cut into bars.

# Cranberry Relish Loaves

1 cup sifted WHEAT FLOUR
1 cup sifted FLOUR
3/4 cup SUGAR
1 Tbsp. BAKING POWDER
1 tsp. SALT
1/2 tsp. BAKING SODA
1/2 tsp. CINNAMON
1/4 tsp. NUTMEG

1 EGG, beaten
2 Tbsp. SALAD OIL
1/2 cup ORANGE JUICE
1 Tbsp. grated ORANGE PEEL
1 cup drained WHOLE
  CRANBERRY SAUCE
1/2 cup crushed WHEAT CEREAL
1/2 cup RAISINS

In a bowl, mix together flours, sugar, baking powder, salt, baking soda, cinnamon and nutmeg. In a separate bowl, combine egg, oil, orange juice, orange peel and cranberry sauce. Combine mixtures and stir in wheat cereal and raisins. Pour into a greased 9 x 5 loaf pan and bake at 350° for one hour.

## Cranberry Bogs

*Cranberries do not grow in water. They are grown in sandy bogs. Because cranberries float, some bogs are flooded when the fruit is ready for harvesting.*

# Cranberry Oat Muffins

1 cup WHOLE-WHEAT
  FLOUR
1/2 cup FLOUR
1 cup QUICK OATS
1 Tbsp. BAKING POWDER
1 tsp. SALT
1/2 tsp. CINNAMON

1 EGG, beaten
4 Tbsp. BUTTER, melted
1 cup MILK
1/2 cup packed BROWN
  SUGAR
1 cup CRANBERRY SAUCE
1 cup chopped NUTS

In a large mixing bowl, combine flours, oats, baking powder, salt and cinnamon. In a smaller bowl, combine egg, butter, milk, brown sugar and cranberry sauce. Combine mixtures until just moistened. Stir in chopped nuts. Spoon into greased muffin pans. Bake at 375° for 20 minutes.

# Cranberry Orange Muffins

1 can (6 oz.) frozen ORANGE
    JUICE CONCENTRATE
2 1/2 Tbsp. SUGAR
2 1/2 cups FLOUR
1/3 cup SUGAR
1 tsp. SALT
1 Tbsp. BAKING POWDER
1 tsp. BAKING SODA

1 cup chopped PECANS
ZEST of 2 ORANGES
1 cup WHOLE BERRY
    CRANBERRY SAUCE
2/3 cup fresh ORANGE JUICE
1 Tbsp. LEMON JUICE
2 EGGS
1/4 cup OIL

Prepare muffin pans by spraying with nonstick spray. Spoon one teaspoon frozen orange juice into each muffin tin, then sprinkle about one-half teaspoon sugar in each muffin tin over the frozen orange juice. Set pans aside until ready to cover with batter. In a large bowl, mix together the flour, sugar, salt, baking powder, baking soda, pecans and orange zest. In a smaller bowl whisk together the cranberry sauce, orange and lemon juices, eggs and oil.

Pour the moist ingredients into the dry ingredients and stir quickly to blend. Spoon into prepared muffin tins filling 3/4 full. Bake on center shelf of 375° oven until brown (25-28 minutes). After removing from the oven, allow to stand a few minutes, then turn pans upside down so muffins will be upside down on waxed paper. Remove any remaining orange and sugar mixture with a spoon and add it to the muffins.

### Cranberries are Healthy, Too!

*Cranberries have been shown to be an effective aid in combatting urinary tract infections. Cranberries also help with blood purification and kidney stone prevention. Note: Do not use sweetened cranberry juice for treating urinary tract infections.*

# Cranberry Date Loaves

**2 cups FLOUR**
**2/3 cup SUGAR**
**1 tsp. BAKING SODA**
**1/2 tsp. SALT**
**1 cup BUTTERMILK,**
**    or YOGURT**

**2 EGGS, beaten**
**3/4 cup SALAD OIL**
**1 Tbsp. grated ORANGE PEEL**
**1 cup chopped DATES**
**1 1/2 cups chopped CRANBERRIES**
**1 cup chopped WALNUTS**

In a bowl, mix together the flour, sugar, baking soda and salt. In another bowl, mix together buttermilk, eggs, oil and orange peel. Combine mixtures until just moist and stir in dates, cranberries and walnuts. Spoon into 4 greased 6 x 3 loaf pans. Bake at 350° for 50 minutes.

# Cranberry Scones

**2 1/2 cups FLOUR**
**2 tsp. BAKING POWDER**
**1 tsp. BAKING SODA**
**1/2 cup SUGAR**
**6 Tbsp. BUTTER**
**1/2 cup DRIED CRANBERRIES**
**1 EGG, beaten**
**1/2 cup PLAIN YOGURT**
**zest of 1/2 LEMON**
**CINNAMON/SUGAR mixture for top**

Preheat oven to 425°. Sift first 4 ingredients together. Cut in butter until mixture is crumbly. Add cranberries, egg, yogurt and lemon zest. Blend all well to make a dough that barely holds together. Press dough out on a floured board. Cut out dough into 1/2-inch thick round or square shapes, about 2 inches wide. Place an inch apart on lightly greased cookie sheets. Bake 10-12 minutes or until lightly golden and well-risen. Sprinkle tops with cinnamon/sugar mixture.

# Cranberry Apple Pie

1 cup CRANBERRIES
3 cups peeled, sliced APPLES
1 cup SUGAR

2 Tbsp. FLOUR
1/8 tsp. SALT
2 Tbsp. BUTTER

Prepare **Orange Pastry** below. Combine cranberries, apples, sugar, flour and salt; mix well. Turn into pastry-lined pie pan, dot with butter. Add top crust. Cut vents in top. Flute edges. Bake in 400° oven 50 minutes or until apples are tender.

## Orange Pastry

2 cups FLOUR
1 tsp. SALT
2/3 cup SHORTENING

1 tsp. grated ORANGE PEEL
1/3 cup ORANGE JUICE

Sift flour and salt. Cut in shortening until crumbly. Add orange peel and orange juice. Toss together with fork until flour is moistened. Form into a ball. Divide in half. Roll out one half on floured surface to fit 9-inch pie pan. Roll our remaining half to use as top crust.

# Apple
# Cranberry Relish Pie

6 cups peeled, sliced APPLES
1/3 cup CRANBERRY RELISH, canned or frozen (thawed)
3/4 cup SUGAR
1 1/2 Tbsp. CORNSTARCH
1/8 tsp. CINNAMON
1 (9-inch) unbaked PIE SHELL

Combine apples, cranberry relish, sugar, cornstarch and cinnamon. Turn into pie shell. Bake in 400° oven 45 minutes or until apples are tender.

# Cranberry Apple Crisp

4 1/2 cups peeled, sliced APPLES
3/4 cup WHOLE CRANBERRY SAUCE
3/4 cup FLOUR
1 cup packed BROWN SUGAR
1 tsp. CINNAMON
6 Tbsp. BUTTER

Arrange apples in a greased 8-inch baking dish. Spread cranberry sauce on top. Combine flour, brown sugar and cinnamon. Cut in butter until crumbly. Sprinkle over apple mixture. Bake in 350° oven for 35-40 minutes or until apples are tender. Serve warm or cold.

# Cranberry Caramel Cake

**Cake:**
1 cup SUGAR
3 Tbsp. BUTTER
1 cup MILK
2 cups FLOUR

2 tsp. BAKING POWDER
1/2 tsp. SALT
2 cups fresh CRANBERRIES
1/2 cup chopped PECANS

**Caramel sauce:**
1 cup packed LIGHT BROWN SUGAR
1 cup BUTTER
1 cup SUGAR
2 cups HEAVY WHIPPING CREAM

Cream butter and sugar; add milk alternately with sifted dry ingredients. Stir in whole cranberries, which have been washed, drained and lightly floured. Add pecans. Pour into a greased and floured 11 x 7 baking dish. Bake at 350° for 25-30 minutes. While cake is baking, prepare caramel sauce: In a saucepan, combine brown sugar, 1 cup butter, sugar and whipping cream. Bring to a boil, stirring well. Serve warm over warm cake.

# Cranberry Raisin Bread Pudding

**Bread Pudding:**
  1 lb. loaf CINNAMON-RAISIN BREAD, sliced
  1 qt. MILK
  3/4 cup packed LIGHT BROWN SUGAR
  2 Tbsp. grated LEMON PEEL
  1 Tbsp. VANILLA
  5 lg. EGGS
  2 APPLES, cored and cubed
  1 cup CRANBERRIES, coarsely chopped
  1/2 cup chopped WALNUTS

**Cider Sauce:**
  3 cups APPLE CIDER
  1 Tbsp. CORNSTARCH, dissolved in 1 Tbsp. WATER
  2 Tbsp. HALF and HALF

Heat oven to 200°. Lay bread slices on racks in oven and bake until dry, but not toasted, about 15 minutes. Remove from oven. Set aside. Increase oven temperature to 350°. Grease a 10-inch tube pan. In small saucepan, combine milk, brown sugar, grated lemon peel and vanilla. Heat on low, stirring, until sugar dissolves. Remove from heat. In large bowl, beat eggs until frothy; slowly stir in milk mixture. Tear bread into small pieces and add to liquid mixture. Stir in apples, cranberries and walnuts until blended. Set bread pudding mixture aside 5 minutes or until bread absorbs most of liquid and softens. Spoon into prepared pan and bake 40-45 minutes. While pudding is cooling, prepare cider sauce: In saucepan, simmer cider until reduced to 1 1/2 cups. Stirring constantly, add cornstarch mixture. Bring to a boil and cook until thickened. Remove from heat and stir in half and half. Turn pudding out onto plate and serve with cider sauce.

# Cranberry Raspberry Sorbet

2 pkgs. (12 oz. ea.) fresh CRANBERRIES
4 fresh ORANGES, peeled, sectioned
2 pkgs. (12 oz. ea.) frozen RASPBERRIES
2 cups SUGAR

Clean cranberries in water, discarding stems and poor, soft berries. Put in food processor bowl with the orange sections and blend thoroughly. Force the mixture through a sieve to eliminate seeds. Process the raspberries and sieve the seeds. Mix the two together, add sugar to taste and process. In a shallow dish, freeze the mixture until nearly solid. Process the semi-frozen mixture to lighten and increase smoothness. Return mixture to dish and refreeze. Shortly before serving, remove from freezer.

# Cranberry Orange Sherbet

1 env. UNFLAVORED GELATIN
1/2 cup COLD WATER
1 lb. fresh CRANBERRIES
2 cups SUGAR
1/2 cup fresh ORANGE
   JUICE
2 cups WATER
1 1/2 cups LIGHT CREAM

Soften gelatin in 1/2 cup cold water. Combine cranberries, sugar and orange juice with two cups water in a saucepan. Bring to a boil and cook until cranberries pop. Add gelatin mixture and stir until completely dissolved. Remove from heat and cool. Pour cooked mixture (a little at a time) into a blender and blend until smooth. Add cream and continue blending. Pour mixture into refrigerator tray and freeze until slushy. Remove from tray and beat mixture at high speed until thick and creamy. Return to refrigerator tray and freeze until firm.

Makes about 2 quarts.

# Variety Berries

# Boysenberry Mint Frosty

1 cup VANILLA ICE CREAM or FROZEN YOGURT
1 cup MILK
1 cup fresh BOYSENBERRIES
1 cup 7-UP® or LEMON-LIME CARBONATED DRINK
MINT LEAVES

Combine ice cream, milk, berries and soda in a blender. Process until smooth and frothy. Garnish with mint leaves.

# Boysenberry Syrup

2 cups fresh BOYSENBERRIES
3 cups WATER
2 WHOLE CINNAMON STICKS
1/2 cup MOLASSES
1/2 cup packed LIGHT BROWN SUGAR
2 tsp. VANILLA

Place berries, water and cinnamon sticks in a small saucepan. Cook over low heat for about 20 minutes. Remove cinnamon sticks and strain. Add remaining ingredients. Cool.

# Boysenberry Custard Pie

2 EGGS, slightly beaten
1/3 cup SUGAR
1/2 tsp. VANILLA
1 1/2 cups MILK, heated
1 can (16.5 oz.) BOYSENBERRIES, drained
NUTMEG
1 (8-inch) baked PIE SHELL

Combine eggs with sugar and vanilla. Add heated milk, beating constantly. Pour into lightly greased 8-inch pie pan. Spread boysenberries over top. Sprinkle with nutmeg. Bake at 350° for 25-30 minutes. Custard should be soft in center—it will set. Cool quickly. Run a knife around the edge and slide custard into baked pie shell.

# Boysenberry Cream Pie

1/2 cup melted BUTTER
2 cups chopped GRANOLA
1 cup flaked COCONUT
1/3 cup ROLLED OATS
4 cups BOYSENBERRIES

3/4 cup + 2 Tbsp. SUGAR
3 Tbsp. CORNSTARCH
dash of LEMON JUICE
1 cup WHIPPING CREAM

Create the pie crust by combining the butter, granola, coconut and oats, mixing well and pressing into an 8-inch pie tin. Bake crust at 400° for 10 minutes. Sprinkle 2 cups of berries with 2 tablespoons of sugar and set aside. Place remaining berries in a pan and add 3/4 cup sugar; mash berries and stir until sugar begins to dissolve. Add cornstarch. Cook over medium heat until mixture is thick and clear. Cool slightly; add lemon juice. Put uncooked reserved berries in the bottom of pie shell, pour cooked mixture over them. Chill until set. Cover with whipped cream and serve.

> **Boysenberries** *were created by horticulturist Rudolph Boysen in 1923 by crossing a raspberry, blackberry and loganberry. They are shaped like a large raspberry.*

# Loganberry Refresher

1/2 cup SUGAR
1/2 cup WATER
7 cups LOGANBERRIES

2 cups ORANGE JUICE
1/2 cup LEMON JUICE
1 1/2 cups COLD WATER

Combine sugar and water in a small saucepan; cook over medium heat until sugar dissolves, stirring constantly. Remove from heat and chill. Mash berries, then press through a strainer to remove seeds (optional). Combine berries with orange juice and lemon juice. Add sugar syrup and chill until very cold. Before serving, add cold water.

# Loganberry Pie

1 1/2 cups SUGAR
1/3 cup FLOUR
1/2 tsp. CINNAMON

4 cups LOGANBERRIES
2 (9-inch) unbaked PIE CRUSTS
1 1/2 Tbsp. BUTTER

Preheat oven to 425°. Mix sugar, flour and cinnamon. Mix lightly with berries and pour into pastry-lined pan. Dot with butter. Cover with top crust. Make slits in top crust for juices to bubble through. Seal and flute edges. Cover edge with foil to prevent excessive browning. Bake 35 minutes or until crust is nicely brown and juice begins to bubble through slits in crust.

*Loganberries, named after James H. Logan, are a cross between blackberries and red raspberries. They have a unique tart flavor.*

# Veal with Loganberry Piquant Sauce

4 VEAL CUTLETS
1/4 cup PARMESAN CHEESE
1 EGG
1 tsp. WATER

BREAD CRUMBS
1/4 cup BRANDY
3/4 cup LOGANBERRY JUICE
3 dashes ANGOSTURA BITTERS

Trim, flatten and dry veal. Press cheese on each side of all cutlets. Beat egg with water. Dip cutlets in egg mixture and then into bread crumbs. Let dry approximately 10 minutes. Fry veal quickly in a mixture of **OIL** and **clarified BUTTER**. Remove from pan. Pour off all but 1 tablespoon of oil. Deglaze pan with brandy. Add loganberry juice and bitters. Cook sauce quickly until reduced by half, approximately 2 minutes. Lay warm cutlets on a pool of piquant sauce. Serve with fresh vegetables and pasta.

# Gooseberry Chutney

2 qt. GOOSEBERRIES
4 1/2 cups BROWN SUGAR
1 cup CIDER VINEGAR
1 (2-inch) stick CINNAMON

8 WHOLE CLOVES
1/4 tsp. NUTMEG
2 WHOLE ALLSPICE
1/2 cup WATER

Wash berries, remove stems and blossom ends. Place sugar, vinegar and spices together in a large pot, add 1/2 cup water and boil for 5 minutes. Add gooseberries and simmer for 30-40 minutes. When the berries are tender and the syrup is thick, remove cinnamon, cloves and allspice; pour into sterilized jars and process according to manufacturer's directions.

*Gooseberries* are an oval, tart fruit or berry that is closely related to the currant. They may be white, yellow, green or red and have a prickly, hairy or smooth surface.

# Gooseberry Crunch

1 cup FLOUR
3/4 cup ROLLED OATS
1 cup packed BROWN SUGAR
1/2 cup BUTTER, softened
1 tsp. CINNAMON

1 cup SUGAR
2 Tbsp. CORNSTARCH
1 cup WATER
1 tsp. VANILLA
3-4 cups GOOSEBERRIES

Mix together flour, oats, brown sugar, butter and cinnamon until crumbly. Press half of crumbs into 9-inch greased pan. In a saucepan, combine sugar, cornstarch, water and vanilla. Bring to a boil, add gooseberries and cook until clear and thick. Pour over crumb mix and top with remaining crumbs. Bake in 350° oven for 45 minutes or until browned. Cut into wedges and serve warm with whipped cream.

# Lingonberry Muffins

1 cup LINGONBERRIES
3 Tbsp. SUGAR
2 cups FLOUR
3 tsp. BAKING POWDER

1/2 tsp. SALT
1 EGG, well-beaten
1 cup MILK
2 Tbsp. melted BUTTER

Sprinkle fresh lingonberries with sugar and let stand. If canned lingonberries are used, leave out the sugar and just measure one cup of the canned berries, since they are already sweetened. Mix flour, baking powder and salt in a large bowl. Combine egg, milk and butter in another bowl and pour into well in center of dry ingredients. Stir lightly and quickly fold in berries. Batter will be lumpy. Fill greased muffin cups 3/4 full and bake at 400° for 25 minutes.

*Tart red* **lingonberries** *are a member of the cranberry family.* **Huckleberries** *are a small, round fruit that grows on a shrub. Each blue or black berry contains 10 hard seeds.*

# Huckleberry Caramel Sauce

1/4 cup SUGAR
2 Tbsp. CORN SYRUP
1 sm. ONION, sliced
1 Tbsp. minced GARLIC
1 Tbsp. minced SHALLOTS
3 sprigs fresh THYME
4 BLACK PEPPERCORNS

2 WHOLE CLOVES
1 WHOLE CINNAMON STICK
2 BAY LEAVES
1/2 cup PORT WINE
1 1/2 cup thickened STOCK
    or DEMI GLACÉ
1/2 cup HUCKLEBERRIES

In a small saucepan, combine sugar and corn syrup and bring to a boil over medium heat. Add onion, garlic and shallots. Cook over medium low heat until it just begins to darken and turn into caramel. Add herbs, spices and port wine. Reduce until nearly dry. Add game stock and simmer for 15 minutes. Strain through fine mesh strainer or cheesecloth. Add huckleberries; simmer for 5 minutes. Serve over meat or poultry.

# Index

# **Index** (continued)

# Index (continued)

# Resource Contacts

**Gingerich Farms**
P.O. Box 484, Canby, OR 97013
503-651-3742, www.gingerich.com

**Oregon Raspberry & Blackberry Comm.**
**Oregon Strawberry Comm.**
712 NW 4th St., Corvallis, OR 97330
541-758-4043, www.oregon-berries.com

**Berry Works**
712 NW 4th St., Corvallis, OR 97330
541-758-4043, berrywrk@peak.org

**Hurst's Berry Farm**
23301 SW McKibben Rd, Sheridan, OR 97378
www.hursts-berry.com

**Wisconsin Berry Growers Association**
www.wiberries.org

**Wild Blueberry Association of NA**
59 Cottage St., Bar Harbor, ME 04609
1-800-ADD-WILD, www.wildblueberries.com

**California Strawberry Commission**
P.O. Box 269, Watsonville, CA 95077-0269
408-724-1301, www.calstrawberry.com

**Univ. of Illinois at Urbana-Champaign**
www.ag.uiuc.edu

**Florida Strawberry Festival**
P.O. Drawer 1869, Plant City, FL 33564-1869
813-752-9194, www.flstrawberryfestival.com

**Florida Strawberry Growers Assn.**
P.O. Drawer 2550, Plant City, FL 33564
813-752-6822, www.straw-berry.org

**North Carolina Dept. of Agriculture**
P.O. Box 27647, Raleigh, NC 27611
919-733-7125  www.agr.state.nc.us

**North Carolina Blueberry Council**
Contact: Laurie Wood
NCDACS Marketing Specialist
ncs0522@interpath.com

**North American Blueberry Council**
4995 Golden Foothill Pkwy, Suite #2
El Dorado Hills, CA 95762
916-933-9399, www.blueberry.org

**Michigan Blueberry Growers Assn.**
MBG Marketing, P.O. Drawer B
Grand Junction, MI 49056
616-434-6791, www.blueberries.com

## APPLE LOVERS COOK BOOK

Celebrating America's favorite—the apple! 150 recipes for m
and side dishes, appetizers, salads, breads, muffins, cakes, pi
desserts, beverages, and preserves, all kitchen-tested by Shir
Munson and Jo Nelson.

5 1/2 x 8 1/2 — 120 Pages . . . $6.

## BEAN LOVERS COOK BOOK

Recipes featuring beans, lentils and legumes. Provides endl
combinations for appetizers, main dishes, soups, salads a
desserts. Presents beans as fun and flavorful alternatives to m
and poultry. Also includes tips for soaking, cooking and prep
ing beans.

5 1/2 x 8 1/2 — 112 Pages . . . $6.

## CORN LOVERS COOK BOOK

Over 100 delicious recipes! Try *Corn Chowder, Corn Souf*
*Apple Cornbread* or *Caramel Corn,* to name a few. You will fi
a tempting recipe for every occasion in this collection. Inclue
corn facts and trivia too!

5 1/2 x 8 1/2 — 88 pages . . . $6.

## PECAN LOVERS COOK BOOK

Indulge your pecan passion for pralines, macaroons, ice crea
bread pudding, rolls, muffins, cakes and cookies, main dishes a
a wide variety of tantalizing pecan pies. By Mark Blazek.

5 1/2 x 8 1/2 — 120 Pages . . . $6.

## PUMPKIN LOVERS COOK BOO

It's pumpkin time again! More than 175 recipes for soups, brea
muffins, pies, cakes, cheesecakes, cookies, ice cream, and mo
Includes pumpkin trivia!

5 1/2 x 8 1/2—128 Pages . . . $6.